Book 1: 61 Days of Barbee's Index Card Art

By Barbara Ann Sanders Hauenstein

Copyright 2018© Barbara Ann Sanders Hauenstein
All rights reserved.

ISBN-13: 978-1974394883
ISBN-10: 1974394883

Dedication and Acknowledgments

This book is dedicated to my amazing family and friends! Above all, to my dear husband Bruce, who's been super supportive – you can do anything and continually bring me joy! You organized this book and got it out of my imagination and into reality. My mother and father were kind, wonderful people, always encouraging me to do my best at whatever made me happy and to help others. My brother Gary is a fantastic artist, detail-oriented with a love of life, people, trivia, art and architecture. As a child, I loved to copy the art you made and learned a great deal from you.

I also dedicate this to the four remarkable sons in our family, Steve, Keith, Robert and Erik and their smart, beautiful, loving wives Sandi, Linda, Tiffany, fiancé Jessica, and children. I continue to be amazed at how much I learn from you!

Cousins Jeannine, Lou, Lauri, Paul, Charm, Diane, Larry, Scott, Don, Juanita, Blair, Betty and families have been there through thick and thin and it means the world to me that we've kept in touch. You encourage me with your daily FaceBook posts and our visits. Bruce's brother Den, wife Nancy, daughters Jen and Tonya, husbands and kids, and sister Sue's sons Brian, Matt, wives and kids and all Bruce's cousins – thank you too for the encouraging FaceBook posts and for keeping in touch! Cousins Laura and Glen, thank you for visiting every Christmas. I've enjoyed our talks more than I can say. It's wonderful to keep our parents' and their relatives' memories alive through our friendship. New-found cousin Kathleen and husband Daniel, it's been amazing to finally meet you.

Fellow artist and friend, Paula Jeffrey (www.paulajeffery.com), author of "61 Rabbits" (Amazon.com) who shared information on how to publish a book, also holds a special place in my heart, as she spurred me on to get this first one finished.

Other great artists influence my daily art and I dedicate this book to them, as well. Tammy Garcia of DaisyYellowArt.com organized the Index Card A Day (ICAD) creative challenge from which these index cards were born in 2017. She contributes time and creative ability to inspire others to create art. Another favorite artist of mine, Carolyn Dube of acolorfuljourney.com and FaceBook Group, "Rediscovering Your Creativity," consistently challenges the imagination and encourages me and many others to create art. My friend, the marvelous Martina, along with Nicole, Milo and Susan, is the humblest of artists, but her warm encouragement and the personalized way she runs her online store MyRustyCrown.com and Facebook Group, "My Rusty Crown Inspiration," has been an inspiration to me and many others. Carol-Ann, Sue, Lisa, Emily, CL, Jane, Angel, Lory, Debbie(s), Leona, Charlene, and Madhumita, your art is fabulous!

My thoughtful neighbors over the past 50 years have provided a wonderful support system throughout my life. Thank you, Ken, Glenn, Glenda, Phyllis, Michelle, Cora, Vinny, Jeff, Erin and all the children and other neighbors for your time and for the Friday afternoon gatherings where some of us solve the world's problems!

Dear friends Lauri, Carolyn and Rosie, plus all my other family, friends and co-workers during my 40+ year career as a logistician, have been my rock and I want to thank them by continuing my life of self-expression.

I post art on buzzybarbee.blogspot.com and several Facebook Groups and enjoy creating art videos. I am committed to encouraging everyone to create and love their own "Happy Art."

Collage of 61 Index Cards

The collage below captures pieces of the complete set of index cards for a summary view. Can you guess which photo goes with which prompt listed in the Table of Contents? The answers lie in the book!

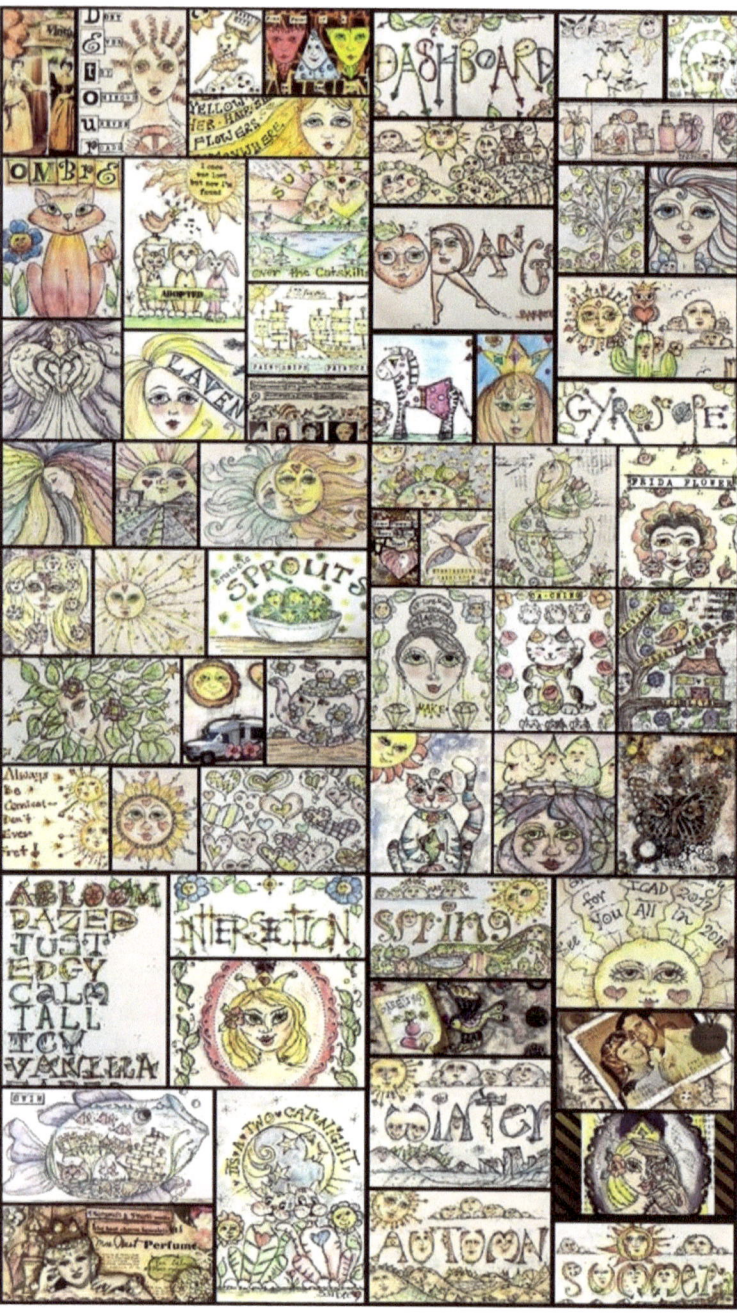

About the Index Card A Day - ICAD - Creative Challenge

I used 4x6 inch thick index cards for each piece, but they may be sized and look slightly different in this book due to publishing requirements.

I've always known that the heavier material of an index card produced great results when I applied more than just pencil to a piece of paper, so I was delighted to find Tammy Garcia's creative index card challenge online in 2015. I joined her ICAD Facebook Group and instantly developed new friendships with her and people from all over the world. It inspired me to do an index card a day during June and July and every summer since. This book is a collection of the cards from 2017. Tammy's amazing ICAD prompts get my creativity flowing. Tammy says it is not an art challenge, but rather a creative challenge to keep you creating something every day. The Facebook Groups have a family-friendly atmosphere, and everyone is warm and helpful. There's no pressure to post art, but it provides a means of communication with others and helps inspire me to continue my commitment to creating daily art.

Tammy's added tips and workshops nudge my creativity. She inspires warmups and tips ahead of the start date to help us prepare for the event. Although there are many materials you can use, common materials that you may already have will get you started. If you are on a budget, gather a pencil, pen (black gel worked best for me), index card, written matter (magazines, newspapers, etc.), glue and/or glue stick, and coloring media (colored pencils, crayons, watercolors, paint brushes, markers, acrylic paint).

In addition to those listed above, my favorite art supplies for this challenge include black waterproof disposable technical pens, black and white paint pens, glitter glue, stencils, rubber or clear stamps, stamp pads, makeup sponges, and old book pages. Any paper with interesting marking (sheet music, texts in different languages, handwriting and scrapbook paper) make a fun background. Matte medium has become a favorite adhesive and overcoat of mine.

I store clean index cards in an inexpensive antique cigar box and finished index cards in a small album rescued from a thrift store. I place it on my living room coffee table and it's a great conversation starter! Each card has the date, prompt and notes on the back.

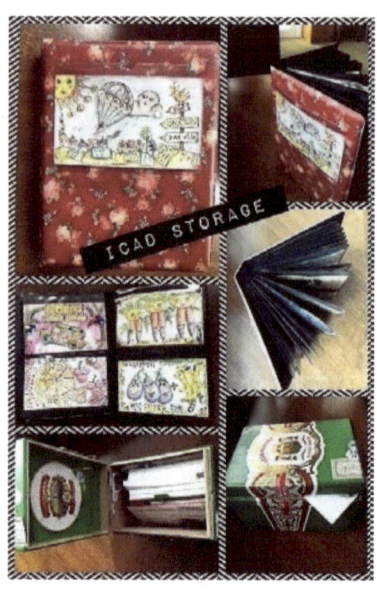

How to Use This Book

I hope you enjoy this book and that it encourages you to create something on a regular basis. It's amazing what you can create just by setting aside 5, 15 (or more) minutes a day and using a minimum of materials. The process engages your mind and body and creates special magical moments that make you forget your daily worries. It helps you enjoy life as it's meant to be enjoyed.

As you wander through this collection of my art, you'll notice there is blank space on some pages. **Please fill it up by doodling whatever comes to mind, including things you see on my cards!** You can view my art videos or look up "how to draw" things you like, and you'll be amazed at what you can do if you try.

My goal in life and with this book is that by getting insight into how I create my art, you too can create, and learn to love, "Happy Art!" More of my art is on my blog at: BuzzyBarbee.Blogspot.com and you may view my videos on my "Barbara Hauenstein" YouTube Channel. Please subscribe to both to make sure you don't miss any new posts and videos!

Table of Contents

Index Cards Created June through July 2017

Copyright ii
Dedication and Acknowledgments iii
About the Index Card A Day (ICAD) Creative Challenge v
Table of Contents vii
01 for 1 June: SUNRISE 1
02 for 2 June: LOST/FOUND 2
03 for 3 June: VINTAGE 3
04 for 4 June: LAVENDER 4
05 for 5 June: KAWAII/CUTE 5
06 for 6 June: DETOUR 6
07 for 7 June: ALLITERATION 7
08 for 8 June: PAINT CHIPS 8
09 for 9 June: OMBRÉ 9
10 for 10 June: SUNSHINE YELLOW 10
11 for 11 June: TETRAHEDRON 11
12 for 12 June: WINGS 12
13 for 13 June: ECHO/REPEAT 13
14 for 14 June: LEAVES 14
15 for 15 June: STARBURST 15
16 for 16 June: RAINBOW 16
17 for 17 June: SPROUT 17
18 for 18 June: ALPHABETIZE 18
19 for 19 June: GEAR OR GADGET 19
20 for 20 June: YIN/YANG 20
21 for 21 June: SIMPLICITY 21
22 for 22 June: VANISHING POINT 22
23 for 23 June: ALICE IN WONDERLAND 23
24 for 24 June: CARAVAN/RV 24
25 for 25 June: PORTRAIT (LEFT+RIGHT) 25
26 for 26 June: GREEN 26
27 for 27 June: FARM (SHEEP) 27

28 for 28 June: DASHBOARD 28
29 for 29 June: POLKA DOTS (PINK TUTU) 29
30 for 30 June: GYROSCOPE 30
31 for 1 July: FAUX WALLPAPER 31
32 for 2 July: DESERT OR DESSERT 32
33 for 3 July: ORANGE 33
34 for 4 July: 4TH OF JULY 34
35 for 5 July: FAVORITE APPLE 35
36 for 6 July: PERFUME 36
37 for 7 July: KAOMOJI OR EMOJI 37
38 for 8 July: CHARCOAL 38
39 for 9 July: AMPERSAND 39
40 for 10 July: STEAMPUNK 40
41 for 11 July: ROOTS 41
42 for 12 July: ONOMATOPOEIA 42
43 for 13 July: LYRICS 43
44 for 14 July: DENIM OR BLUE 44
45 for 15 July: NIGHT SKY 45
46 for 16 July: LOVE 46
47 for 17 July: LAYERS 47
48 for 18 July: INTERSECTION 48
49 for 19 July: CHARM BRACELET 49
50 for 20 July: SUN OR MOON (2-CAT NIGHT) 50
51 for 21 July: SWIM (FISHBOWL) 51
52 for 22 July: ADJECTIVE 52
53 for 23 July: MIRROR 53
54 for 24 July: GREETINGS FROM 54
55 for 25 July: SEPIA (EYES) 55
56 for 26 July: GHOST OR ZOMBIE 56
57 for 27 July: SPRING 57
58 for 28 July: SUMMER 58
59 for 29 July: AUTUMN 59
60 for 30 July: WINTER 60
61 for 31 July: SUNSET 61

01 for 1 June: SUNRISE

For this first prompt of SUNRISE I wanted to incorporate cats and remembered the Catskill Mountains in New York from some far corner of my mind. I don't recall going there so I must've heard about it in school, decades ago! Who says your memory fades with age, ha-ha! I wonder what other important things I'll remember as I get older! I added a red gem on my cat-sun's forehead for good measure.

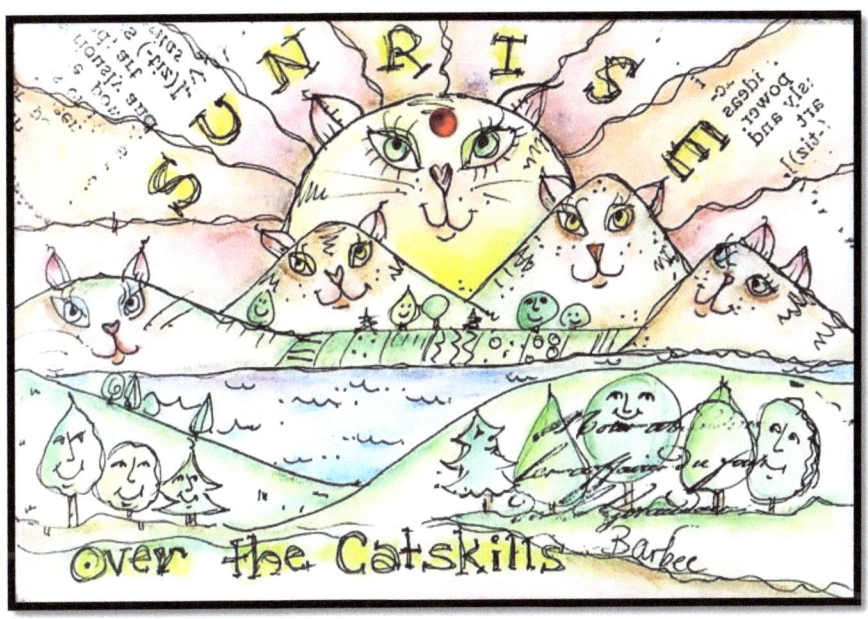

02 for 2 June: LOST/FOUND

This one is for all of us who've either lost and/or found best friends - cats, dogs, rabbits, birds, turtles, snakes, fish, etc. My family has adopted and enjoyed several marvelous pets who've enriched our lives beyond words!

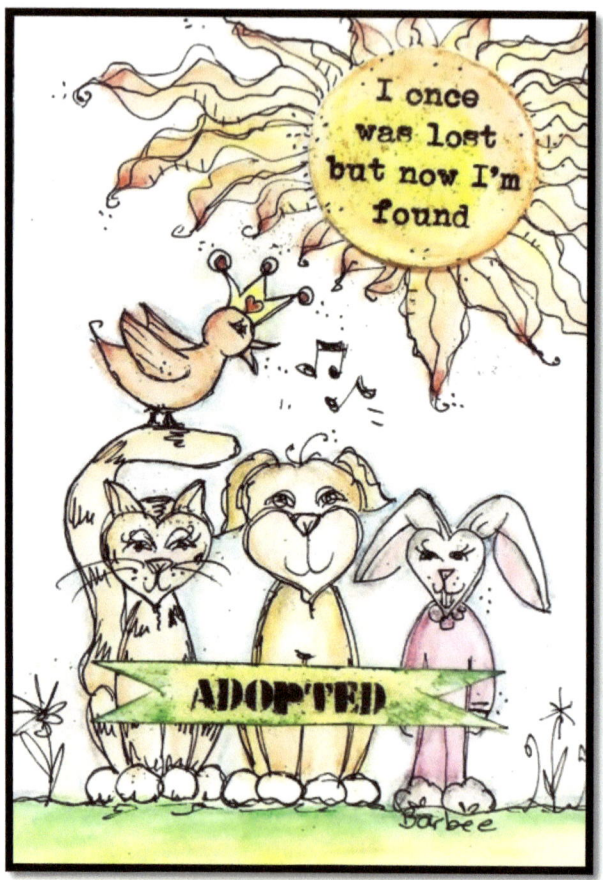

03 for 3 June: VINTAGE

I used several photos gathered from different relatives of my great grandmama, Exilda, for this third prompt, VINTAGE. She had a bit of a Moses story. My dad always talked about his grandmama who'd come over to the Canadian mainland on a ship that sank but she was placed in a life boat and someone found her on the beach, so she was raised there before immigrating to America. As I worked through records of my family, generating a family tree these past few years, there it was on a death certificate, with other records saying the same thing, location of birth: "at sea." In other records, it stated her place of birth as "the Atlantic Ocean!"

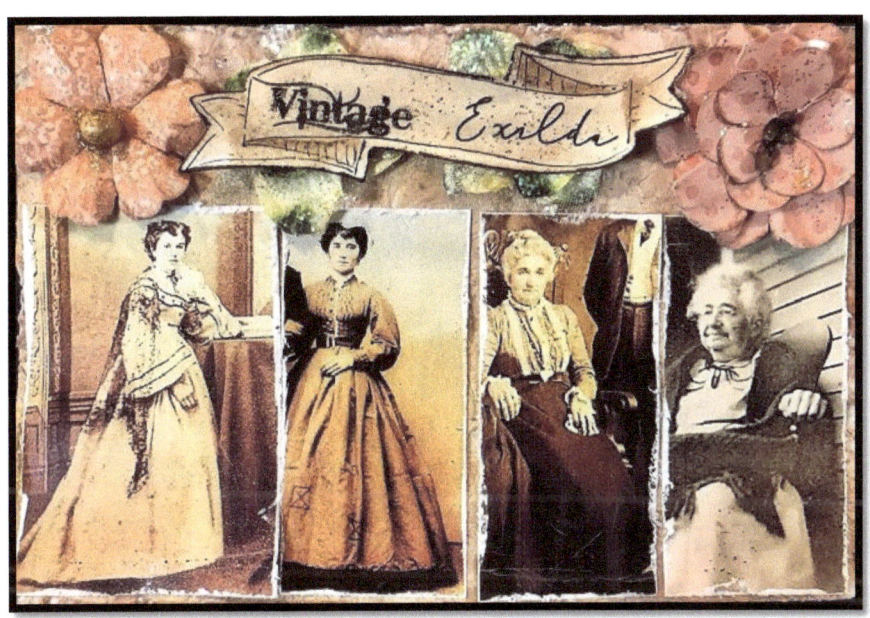

04 for 4 June: LAVENDER

I wanted to draw a face and incorporate a sun-mandala plus a hint of fields of lavender on this card. I love to conduct research for my drawings by looking at various pages on the internet so that I can provide some resemblance to the subject matter! Even so, I own an artist license that allows me to deviate – sometimes quite broadly – from reality!

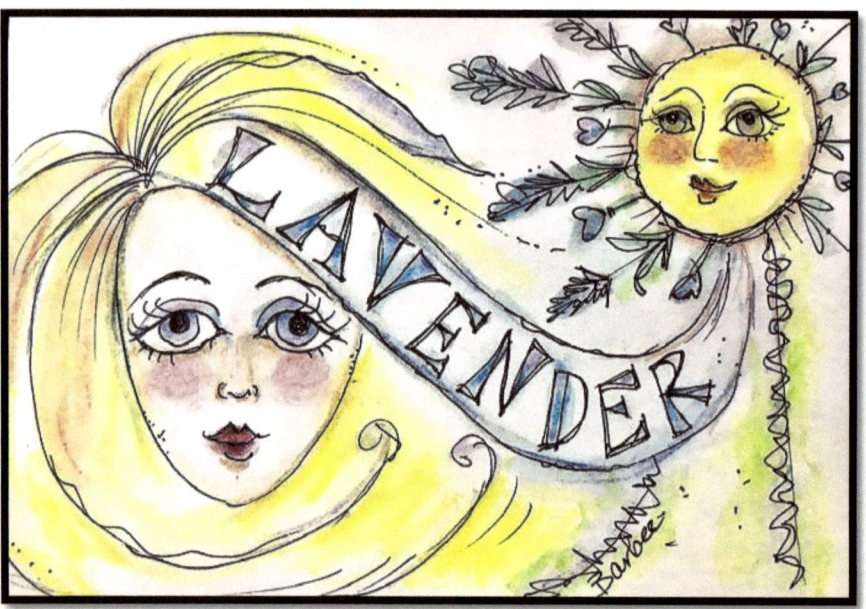

05 for 5 June: KAWAII/CUTE

I'd never heard of the word KAWAII, so this was the perfect opportunity to research it and, in the context of Japanese popular culture, it means: cute, as in "she paints elephants that are extremely kawaii" or as a noun: the quality of being cute, or items that are cute, as in: "even in a cosmopolitan city like Tokyo, kawaii is everywhere."

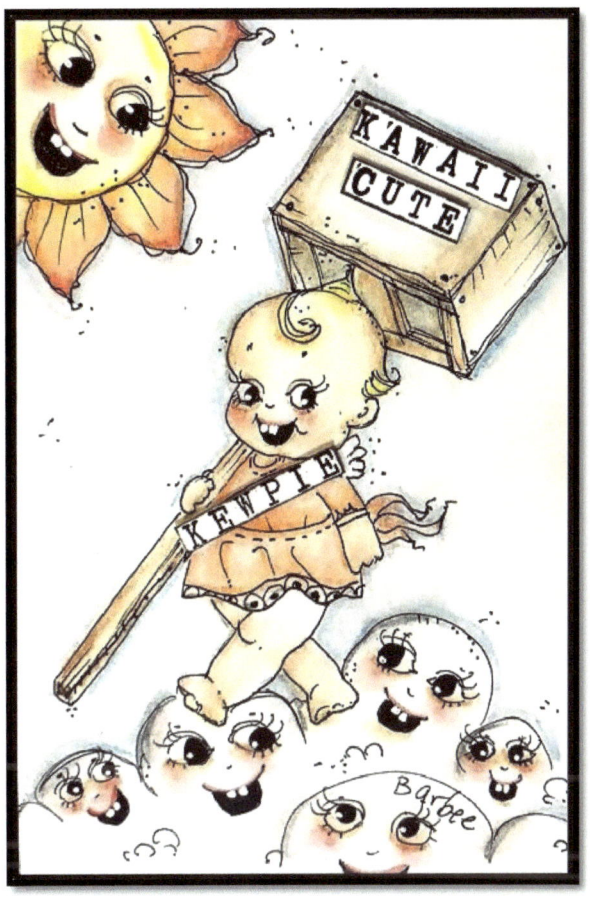

So, I looked at images and there are many, cute kitties, etc., but I thought I'd take inspiration from the Kewpie Doll who had its beginnings in the U.S. around 1909 by an artist named Rose O'Neil. I hope she'll forgive me for personalizing this cute baby by adding teeth and other small adjustments!

You can read more about this in an article that relates it to women suffragettes and helping get women the vote by searching for Kewpie and reading about its creator, Rose O'Neil on the internet.

06 for 6 June: DETOUR

I did a little acrostic poem with this prompt and thought I'd draw a matching drawing. Of course, not everyone looks like this when they encounter a detour, but I was inspired by events that happened when my husband and I drove around the U.S. in our 28-foot motorhome towing a car and came up detours that showed measurements which wouldn't work with our rig and we had to suddenly and swiftly make a decision on what to do. Fortunately, we came out of those events alive, but they were harrowing at times, particularly in New Jersey!

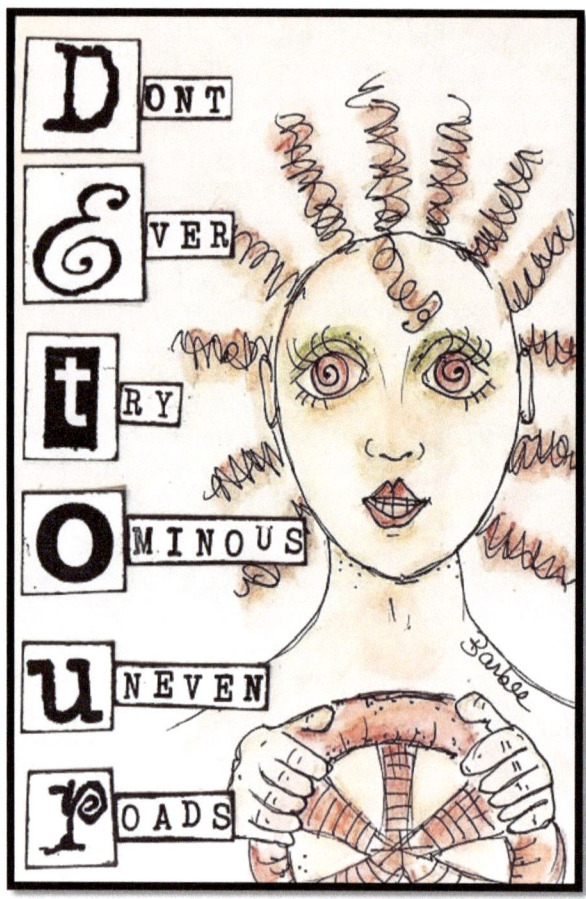

07 for 7 June: ALLITERATION

Unfortunately, I never got to meet my sweet grandma Eva, the daughter of my great grandmama VINTAGE Exilda (card #03). According to my father, Eva had a warm, loving manner and was never mad, impatient or mean. She also loved cats, which is why I wrote this alliteration for her! Her sister-in-law, my dad's Aunt Mildred, loved chickens and I've found old photos of her with the words "she never met a chicken she didn't like" penned on them, giving me the thought that Eva never met a cat she didn't like! I must thank my cousin Betty for these photos! Many were handed down to her and me by my dad's sister, whom I viewed as a sort of Grandma since Eva went on to greener pastures before my birth. This card was collaged with my drawings, stamped text and photos.

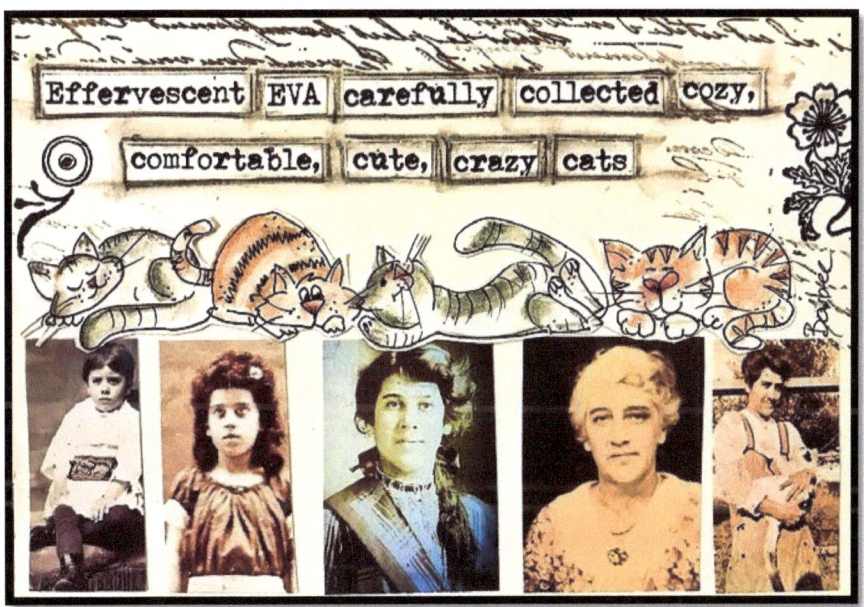

08 for 8 June: PAINT CHIPS

Did someone say, "PAINT SHIPS?" Well, maybe not, but I clipped up some paint chips for the water under my painted ships. Years back, I taught a Columbus Day art lesson for one of my son's 4th Grade Class as part of a volunteer program called "Arts Attack," giving the teacher a break. The class quickly got unruly, but my son told them to pipe down, ha-ha! I got them under control by telling them it was fine for them to ignore my teaching and not do a painting to show their teacher when she returned to see what they'd accomplished. Of course, then they realized their teacher would know they'd misbehaved and completely settled into the art lesson, with some enjoyment, too, I might add. Each ended up with a wonderful piece of art to show their teacher and parents!

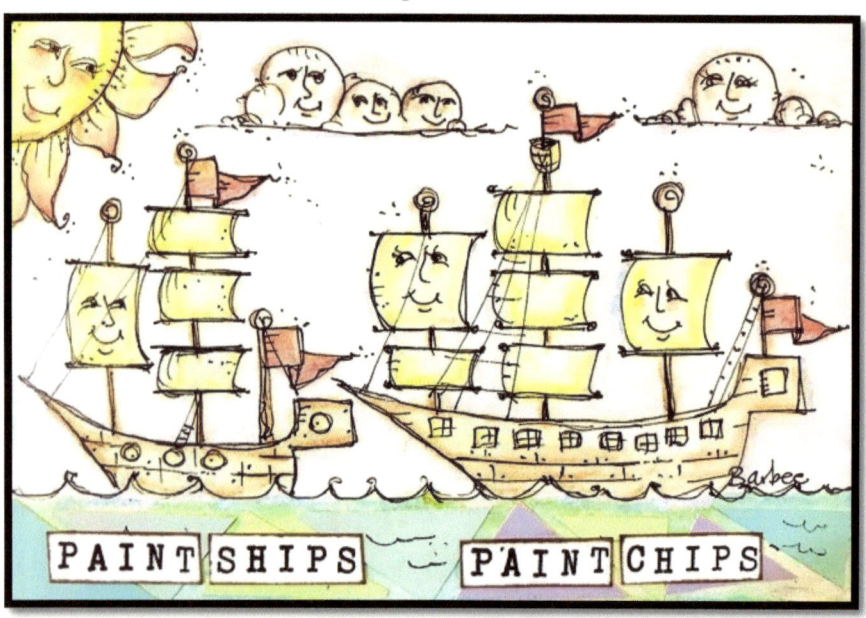

09 for 9 June: OMBRÉ

Here's an OMBRE cat! OMBRÉ means shades, so I tried to get shades of a color, although it's difficult on these index cards which have a thin, rather slick surface compared to the better quality, high priced, thick, tooth-y watercolor paper I normally paint on! That's what using index cards is all about though, it enables you to try new things without fear of ruining good paper and is a bit humbling in the process.

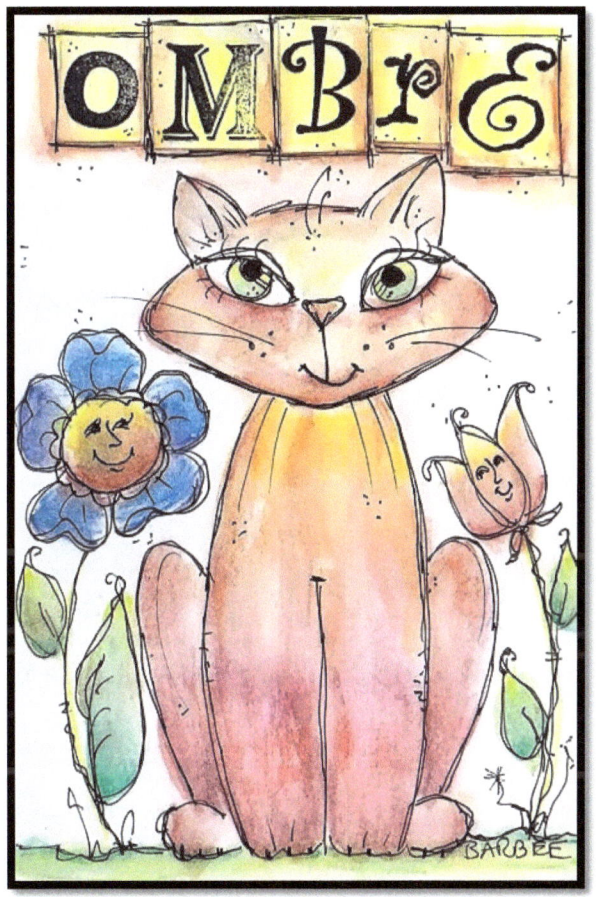

10 for 10 June: SUNSHINE YELLOW

A little rhyme: "Sunshine yellow was her hair, she had flowers everywhere." Which of these yellows do you think is "sunshine" yellow? I had fun playing with watercolors that I received from my dear, thoughtful daughter-in-law for Mother's Day!

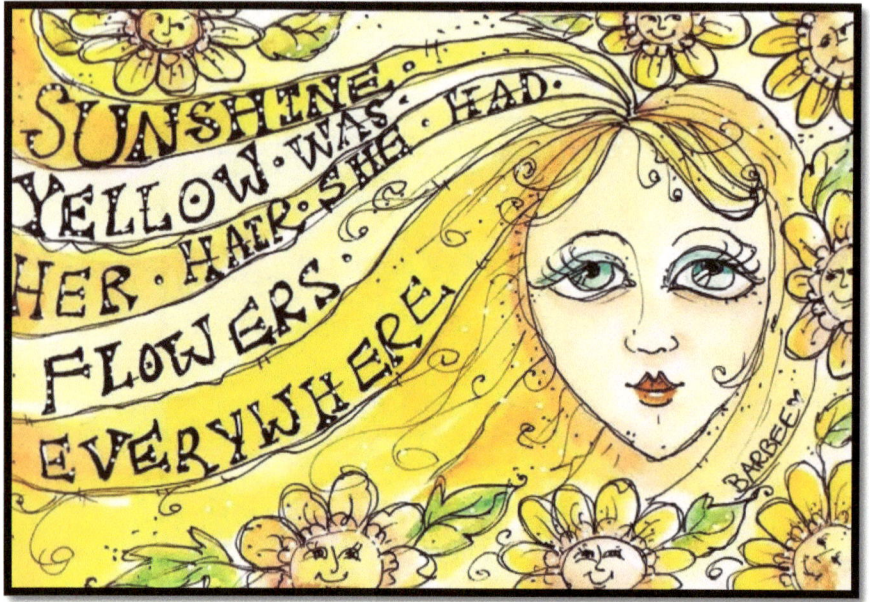

11 for 11 June: TETRAHEDRON

I love following the prompts because I must either dig back into the deep recesses of my mind or conduct research on the internet to get a good perspective. When I heard that a tetrahedron has four faces, I knew I had to draw 4 faces - yay! I started out by painting metallic paints on the card, then stenciled over them with black archival ink as a foundation. I clipped out some triangles and painted, then inked, them into faces before gluing them to the foundation and adding the text.

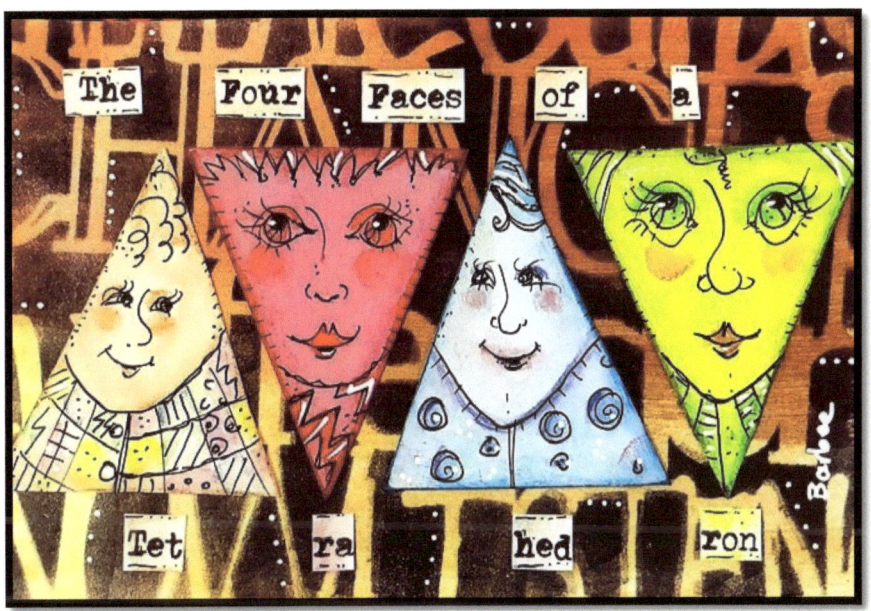

12 for 12 June: WINGS

We flew half-way across the United States while I did this piece, from the southwest-most point to the beautiful Midwest heartland of our country, to see one of our sons get married to his dear love. I have many angels in my life and enjoyed giving this one life on an index card. I must add that the wedding was beautiful and I realized that the purpose of weddings is to setup a network of friends to help the new couple as they tackle life together.

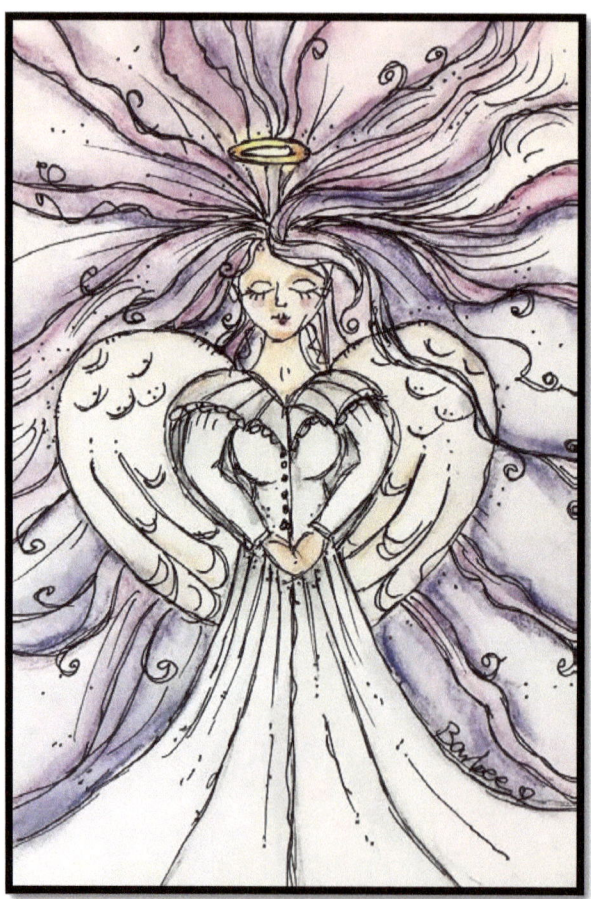

13 for 13 June: ECHO/REPEAT

Every one of us has at least one thing in common - a heart! I repeated the heart symbol many times but they're all different - which one is your favorite? They're like us - different sizes, different colors, evoking different feelings within us. My life's goal is to look deeper than what my eyes see and to look within others' hearts as well as my own, in order to become a better, happier, more helpful person.

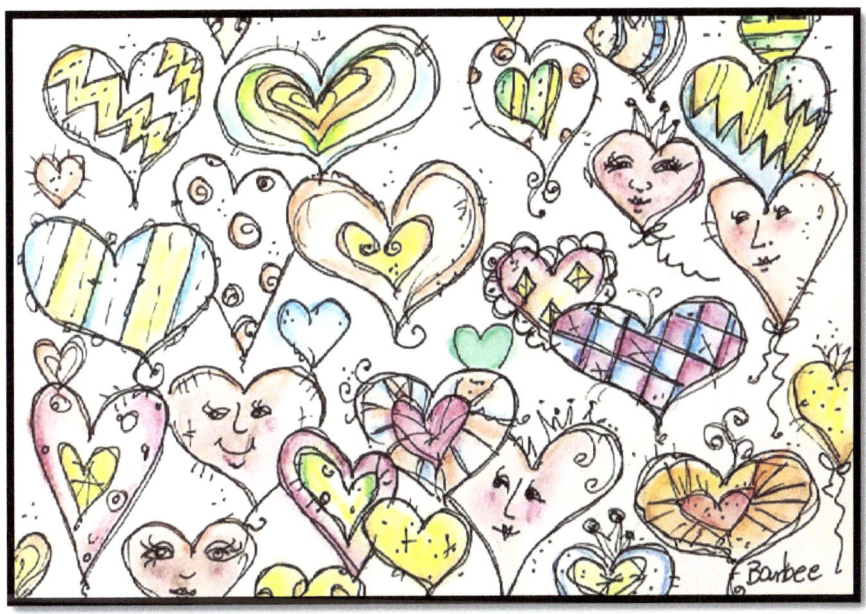

14 for 14 June: LEAVES

I had fun adding leaves to this lady's head, ha-ha! I don't like white space much so added stars on the background, too! I normally have something I want to draw. When I see the prompt for the day, I think about how I can incorporate that drawing into one that portrays the prompt. In this one, I wanted to practice a 3/4 face and simply added leaves for hair and all around. I love drawing faces as much as I do leaves so was happy to draw, then paint, this piece.

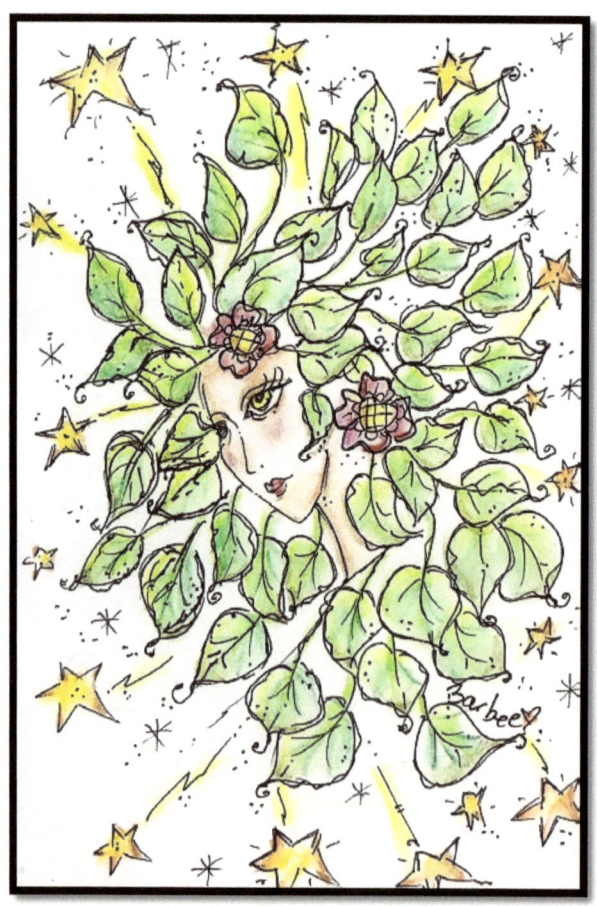

15 for 15 June: STARBURST

I created a sun-starburst-mandala with a happy face for this prompt because I love the sun, stars and mandalas! Mandalas aren't always perfectly symmetrical. I didn't realize till doing this challenge how much an artist's license is worth. It's far more fun to try something new than to repeat something over and over. I also enjoy making things imperfect. My philosophy is that it's impossible for me to see an error if everything is a bit off!

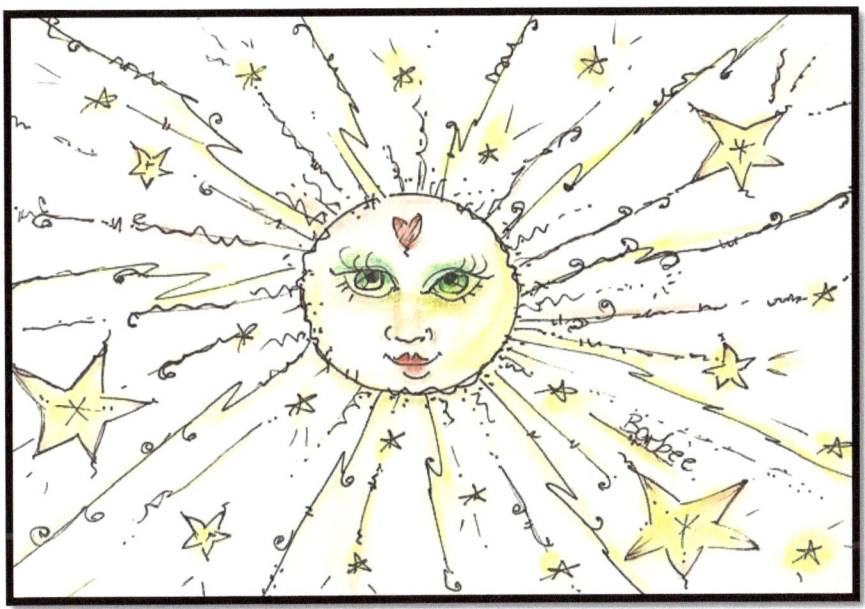

16 for 16 June: RAINBOW

This was fun! I created a RAINBOW Girl using watercolor pencils in order of the way I arrange the colors in my pencil case. I started at the bottom with yellow and went around, ending with charcoal gray and repeating orange to end on a bright note. What's your favorite color? This is another case of wanting to draw a face and applying the prompt to it by incorporating the word in the prompt.

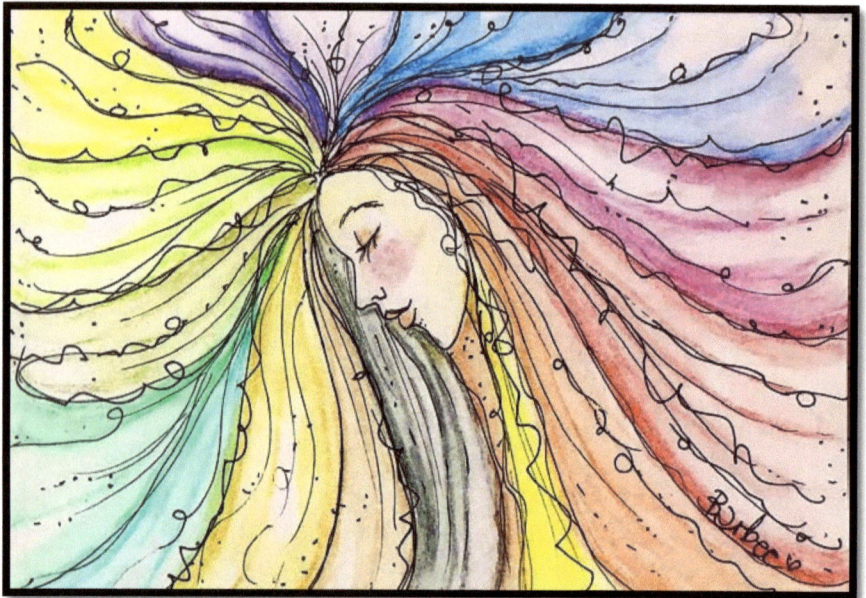

17 for 17 June: SPROUT

Gosh, I LoVe Brussels Sprouts. So, this was where my pencil and pen took me when I saw the prompt, SPROUT! Brussels Sprouts are so cool when you see them on the stalk – lots of photos on the Internet! I decided to do a bowl of them, although, one day I'll create a piece with them on the stalk! I couldn't resist adding faces, as always, too. I kind of like the sleeping one - do you have a favorite?? And my art wouldn't be complete with too much white space so I filled the background with stars.

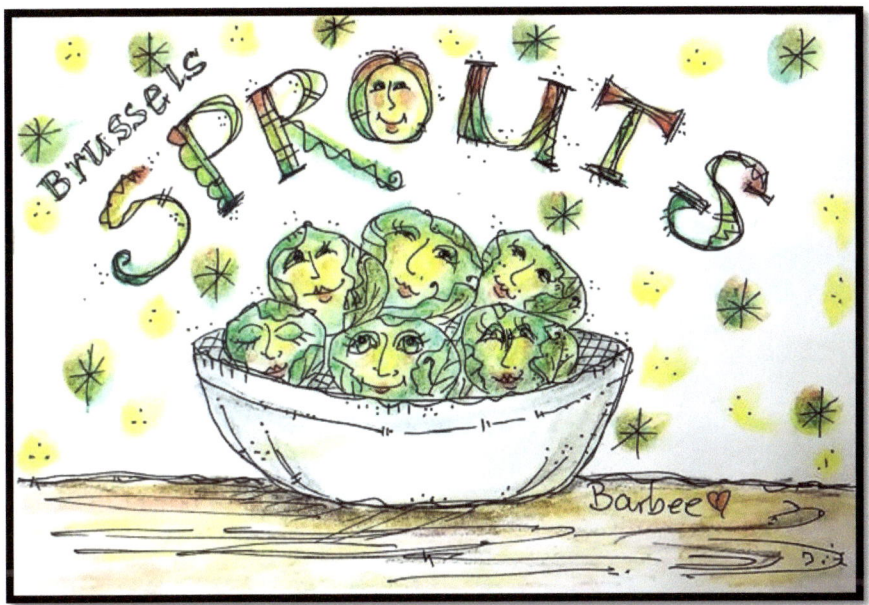

18 for 18 June: ALPHABETIZE

This piece started with the creation of an acrostic-style poem for the first letters of the alphabet which are ALPHABETIZED (ABCDEF). Since the theme for this week involved suns, moons, spheres, mandalas and circles, I randomly drew circles and let my brain guide my art from there! So, we have happy suns and moons with mandala-ish rays and a meaningful alphabetized acronym to boot!

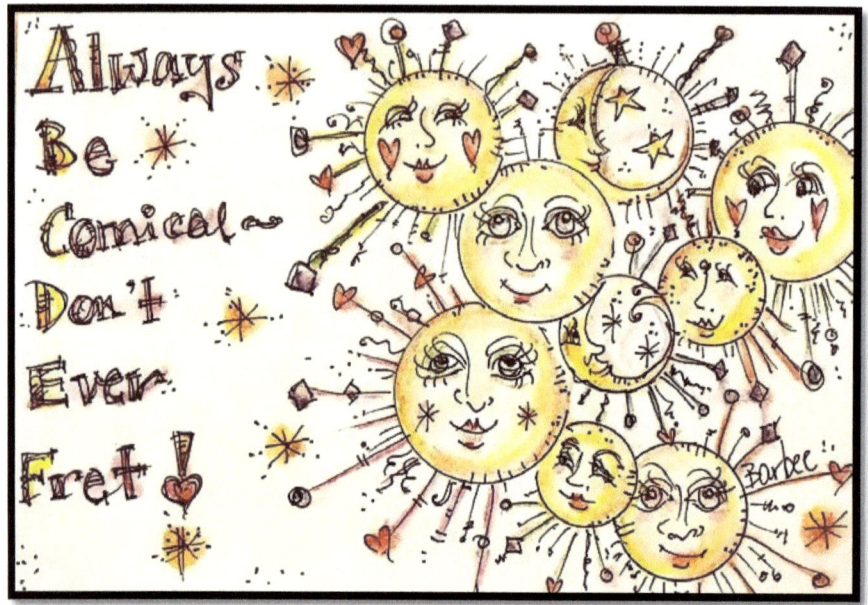

19 for 19 June: GEAR OR GADGET

I created this during our trip from San Diego to Iowa, and randomly placed some things I thought resembled gears and sprockets into it. My husband said they resembled electric razor blades! Well, I guess those are gadgety things too, so they're ok. After drawing her head, I tried to fill the white space with a sun, but I didn't like it, so I cut out the head from the first index card, covered another index card with washi tape and glued the clipped head to the second card. There's always a way to help yourself to like your art a bit more if you feel you've made a mistake or you just don't love it like you want to. I adore steampunk but realize I have a long way to go to be able to portray it, cuz I think she looks more like Frankenstein, but nevertheless, she was fun to do!

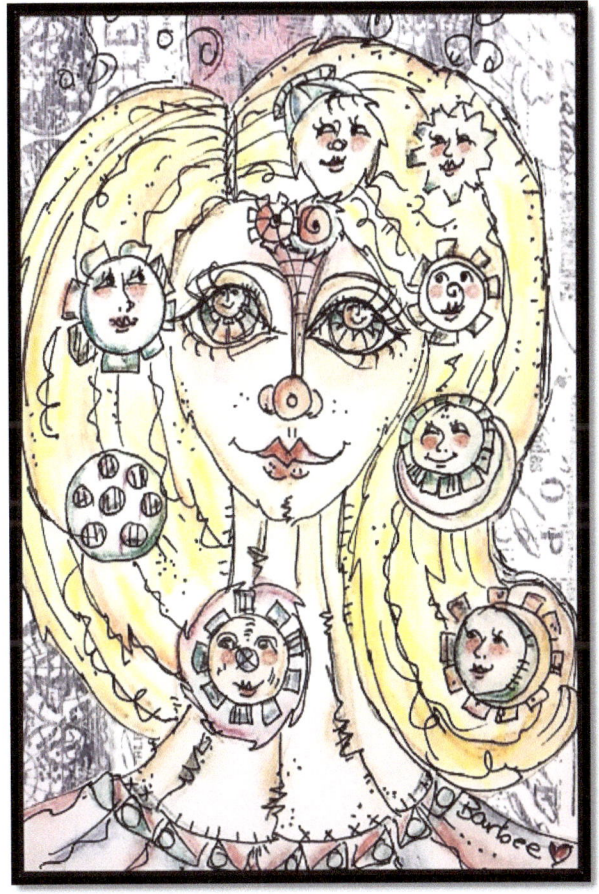

20 for 20 June: YIN/YANG

The definition of yin/yang from dictionary.com is: "(in Chinese philosophy and religion) two principles, one negative, dark, and feminine (yin) and one positive, bright, and masculine (yang) whose interaction influences the destinies of creatures and things." This one reminds me of the close relationship many of us have with our significant other as these two seem very comfortable and happy being so close together.

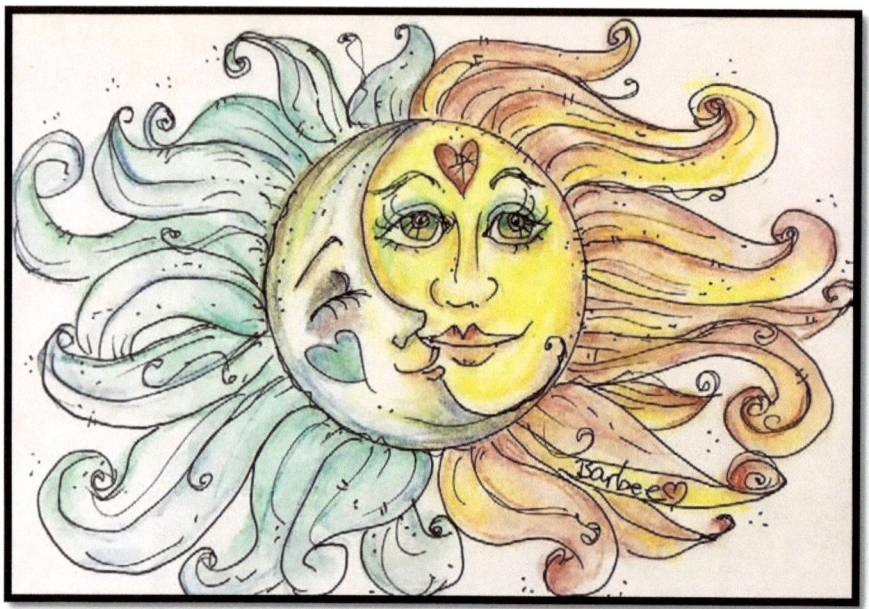

21 for 21 June: SIMPLICITY

I started drawing a sun for this creation and ended up with a more complex sunflower/ mandala. It's interesting where my mind takes me when I start out going in another direction. It's an example of the magical state I get in when I create something fun. Art takes me beyond the worries of life and helps me enjoy all creation much more.

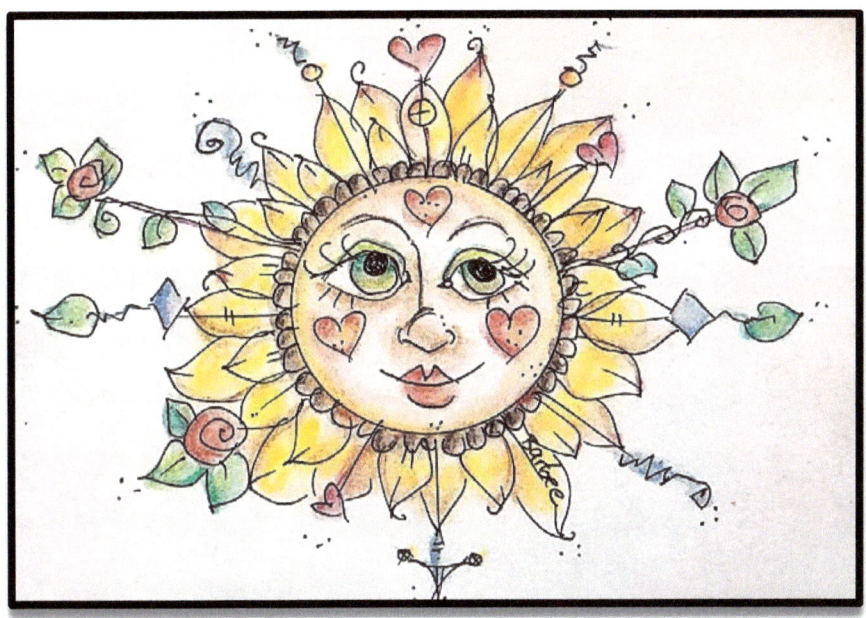

22 for 22 June: VANISHING POINT

Thinking about this prompt, my thoughts wondered around my huge home State of California – from the incredible Imperial Valley to the amazing Salton Sea to the Pacific Coast Northward to the Golden Gate Bridge and beyond! Although I love all our 50 states (having lived in several), California offers phenomenal fruits and vegetables that grow year-round, supplying a large portion of the U.S. and world's food! This amazing state covers a huge amount of diverse land up and down the Pacific Ocean, feeding us fantastic food, without which we wouldn't be as healthy as we are. I enjoyed portraying part of this - from the California/Arizona Border (with those crazy rock and mountain formations) northward to the inland and coastline valleys! I added rows of plants to depict the bounteous crops we grow in our fine state.

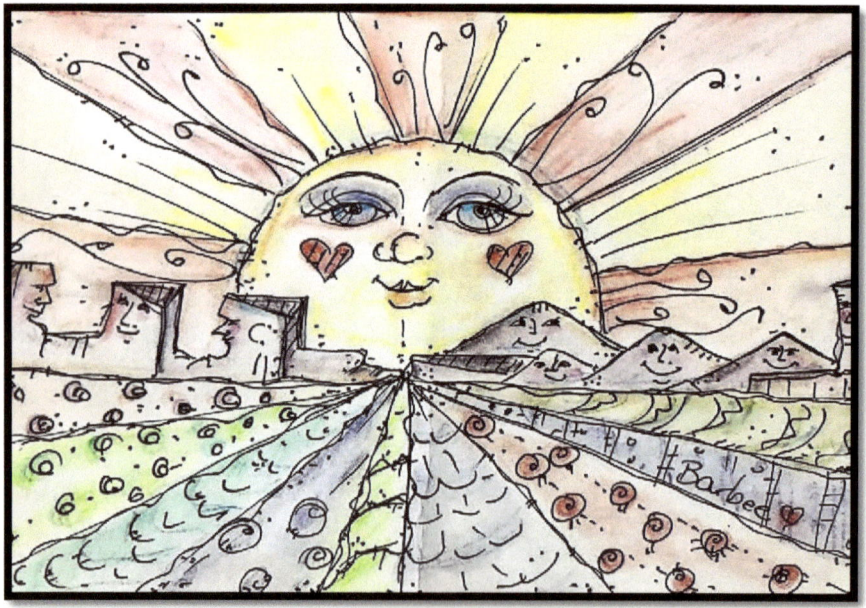

23 for 23 June: ALICE IN WONDERLAND

I drew and colored a teapot with personality with a backdrop of flying cups and flowers for this fun prompt, once again proving, apparently, how much I dislike white space, ha-ha!

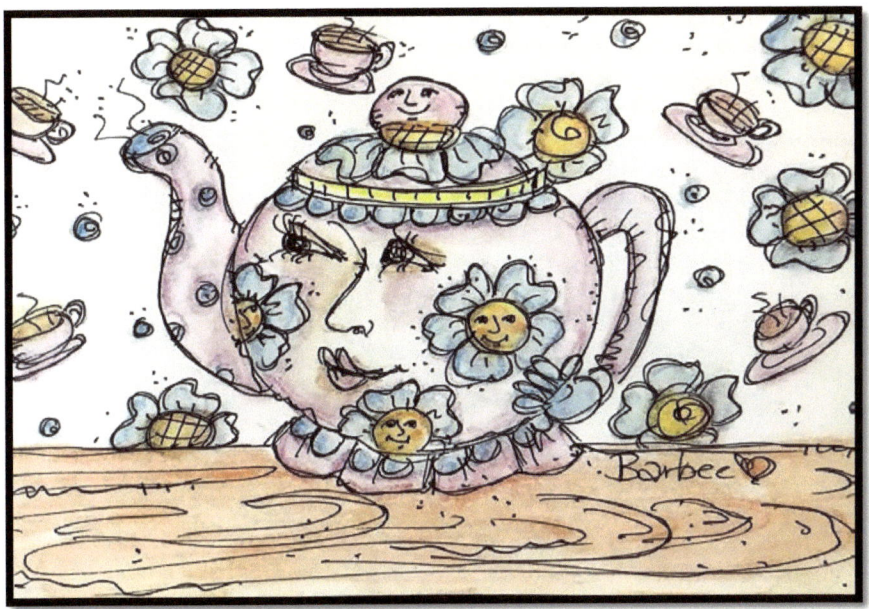

24 for 24 June: CARAVAN/RV

I'm dedicating this to my sweet husband for all he does for me every day. Our 28-foot motorhome, also known as a Recreation Vehicle (RV), has been perfect for seeing the U.S. and Canada and for helping us keep up with our growing family who live all over the U.S. Every trip has been an amazing adventure! I glued this index card onto a greeting card blank and gave it to my husband with a little poem inside the card to thank him for all he does.

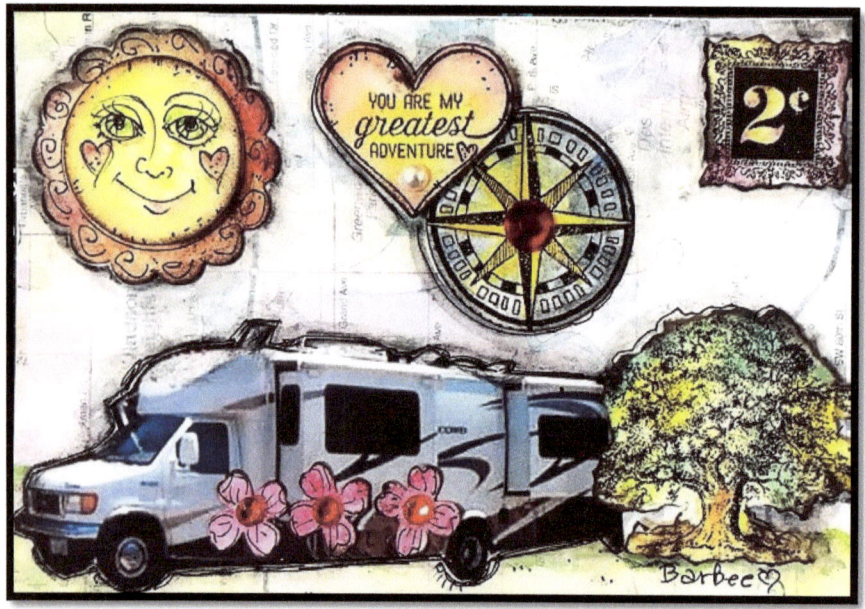

25 for 25 June: PORTRAIT (LEFT+RIGHT)

I wanted to experiment, so taped two 4x6 inch index cards together in the back and drew a portrait with the middle of the union of the two cards in the middle of the face. I traced one side of the face onto the other to see if I could get symmetry, since my faces always seem so lopsided to me! Here's the resulting "doublet."

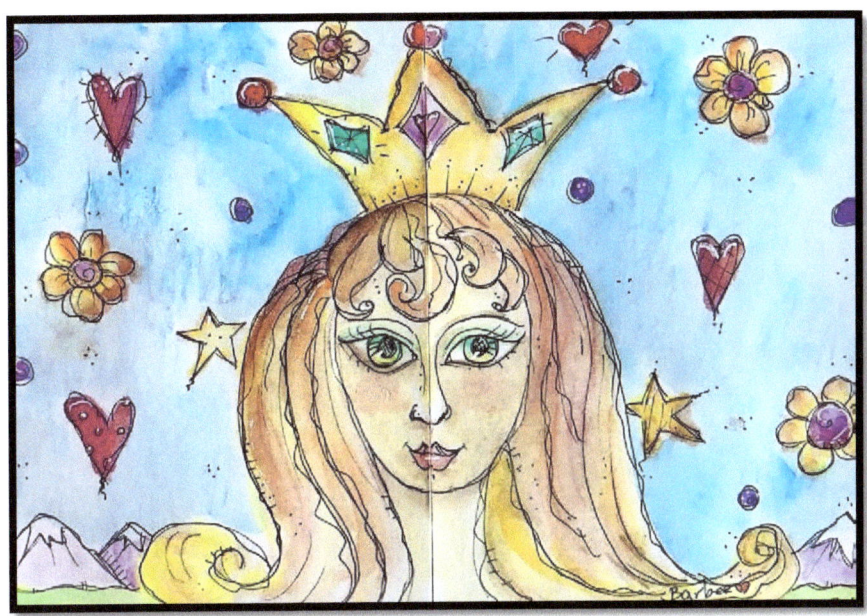

26 for 26 June: GREEN

This cool kitty follows his heart, even though its GREEN, ha-ha! I added a green gem in his heart. By the way, I heard that this is a male because only male cats can be green! This one's dedicated to a dear veterinarian friend, Cora and her husband Vinny, who used to live across the street but recently moved to another state. I still enjoy reading her fun posts on FaceBook!

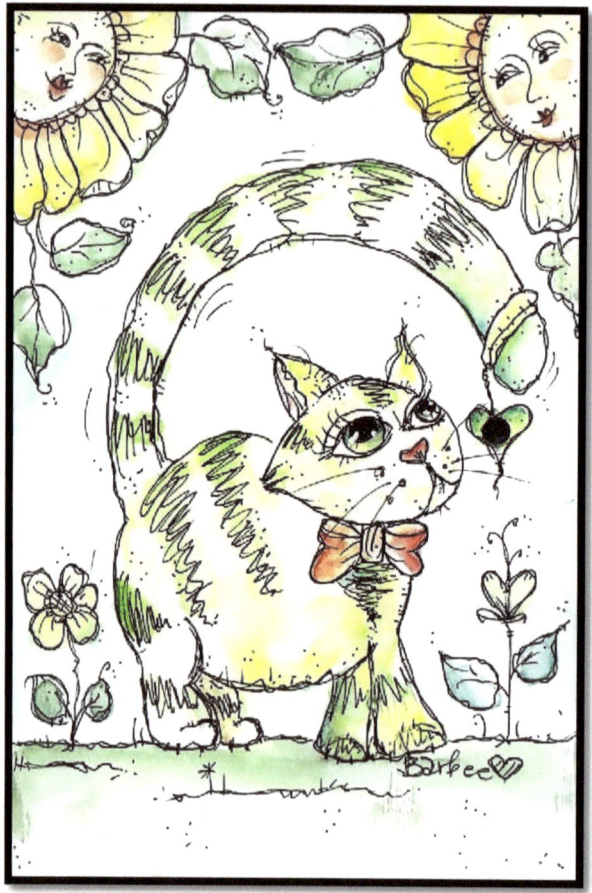

27 for 27 June: FARM (SHEEP)

I started out wanting to do a beautiful huge Amish barn but decided to do some fun, silly sheep instead. It was late at night and they tired of jumping over the same old fence to help me try to sleep so they embarked upon something new. Unfortunately, I then imagined a sheepish sun and sheeply clouds which gave a whole new meaning to puffy clouds, ha-ha! Oh, well, my imaginary sheep had a great time anyway.

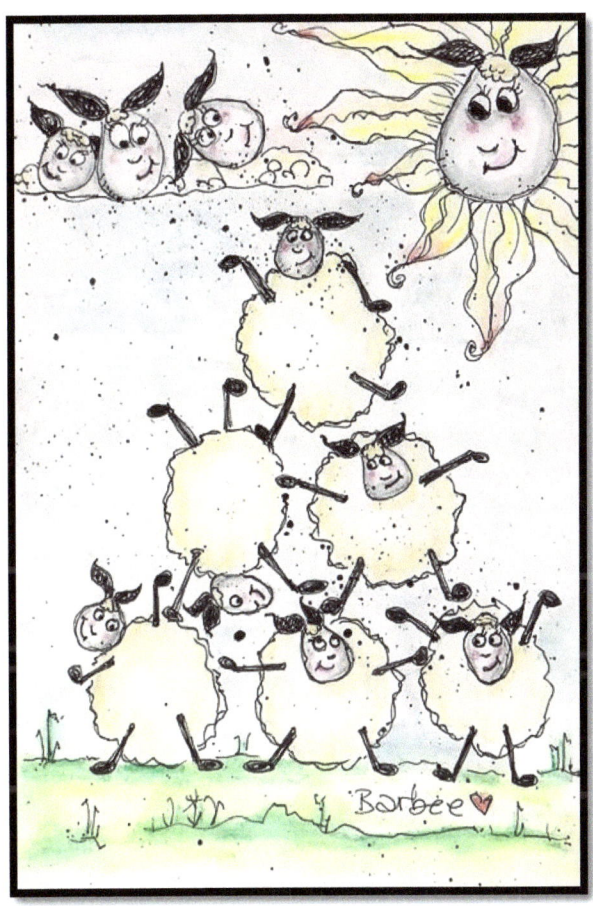

28 for 28 June: DASHBOARD

Before I retired, one of the catchy new things my employer was doing was creating digital dashboards for things like efficiency and performance. You could go to an internet page and see little meters that depicted how you were doing compared to goals of how you should be doing. It was very interesting to see everything in one place. It was a digital report card, and I embraced it as a tool to see how we were doing at metrics that were important to my leadership and me. I decided to portray this using the wonky lettering method for today's prompt, DASHBOARD, but took the opportunity to add some flowers with faces to give the piece some personality.

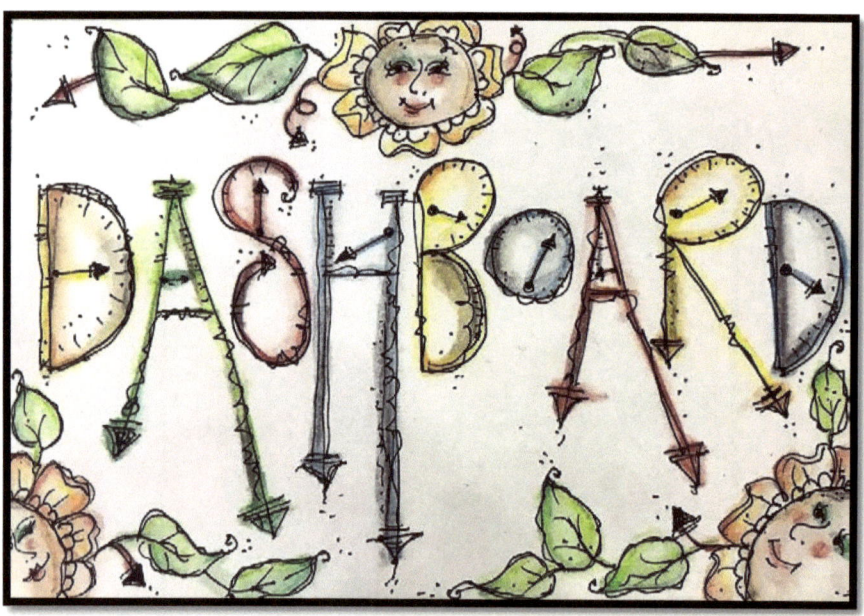

29 for 29 June: POLKA DOTS (PINK TUTU)

If I was a Zebra, I'd want pink polka dots and a pink tutu! This sweet Zebra is asking the age-old question: "do these polka dots make my butt look big!" I began with the idea of having a polka dotted zebra amongst a heard of regular, striped zebras but quickly realized it would be quite difficult to draw all that on a 4x6 inch index card! So, I opted for one "tutu'd" zebra.

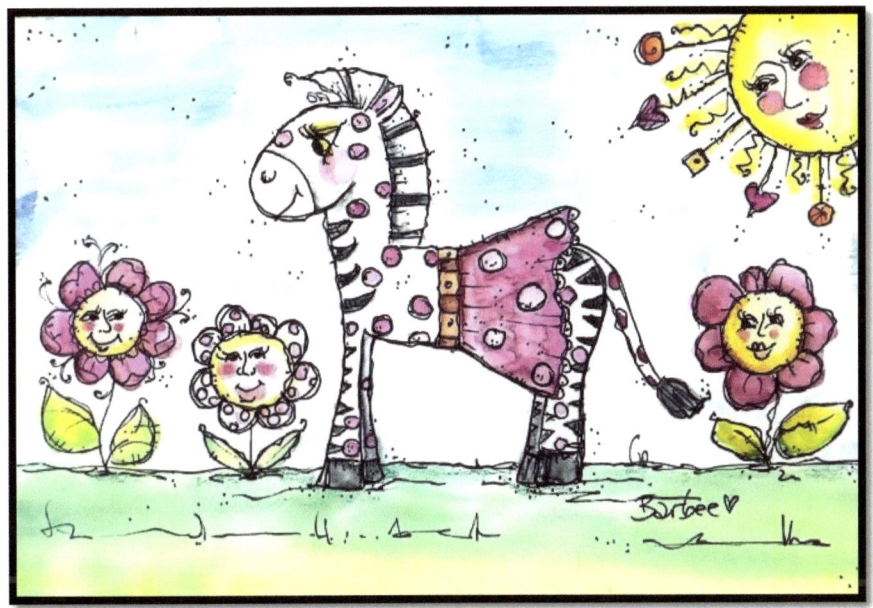

30 for 30 June: GYROSCOPE

I used to repair and overhaul aircraft gyroscopes during my time as an aircraft instrument mechanic apprentice in the early 1980s. So, it was quite interesting when, in the early 2000s, I got my last job as a group supervisor and was told by a person of equal rank on a different subject that I'd done an excellent demonstration for him during that old job! Wow, I always found gyros so difficult, but that was such a nice compliment that I tried to stop being so negative about things! I hope everyone recognizes the beauty and quality of their work and is kinder and gentler on themselves.

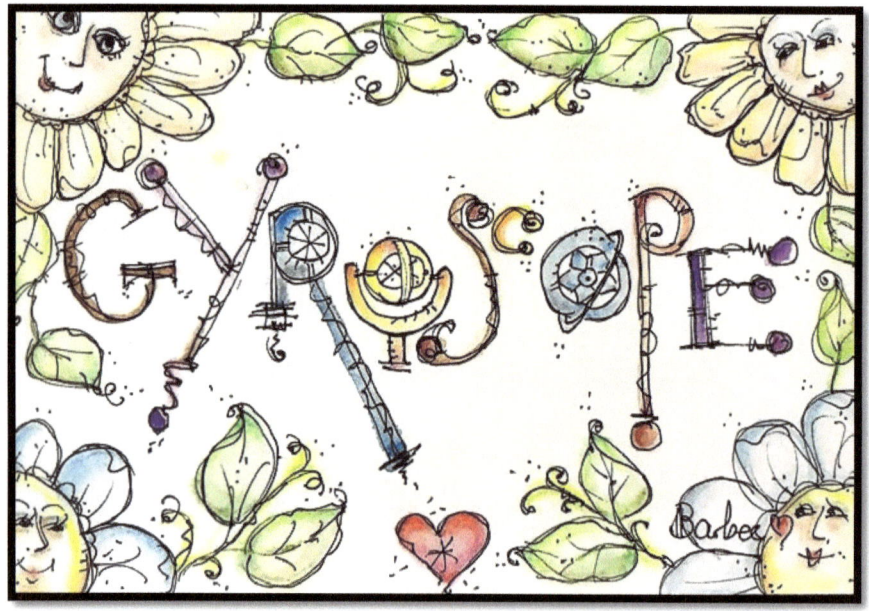

31 for 1 July: FAUX WALLPAPER

I loved seeing the beautiful swatches of "wallpaper" (plots of land) from our airplanes when we flew to the Midwest to see one dear son marry his soulmate and we were very fortunate to have two of his three brothers, with their families, attend. These beautiful patches of land reminded me of a patchwork of wallpaper, so I drew that for this prompt, incorporating feelings from my trip into my art.

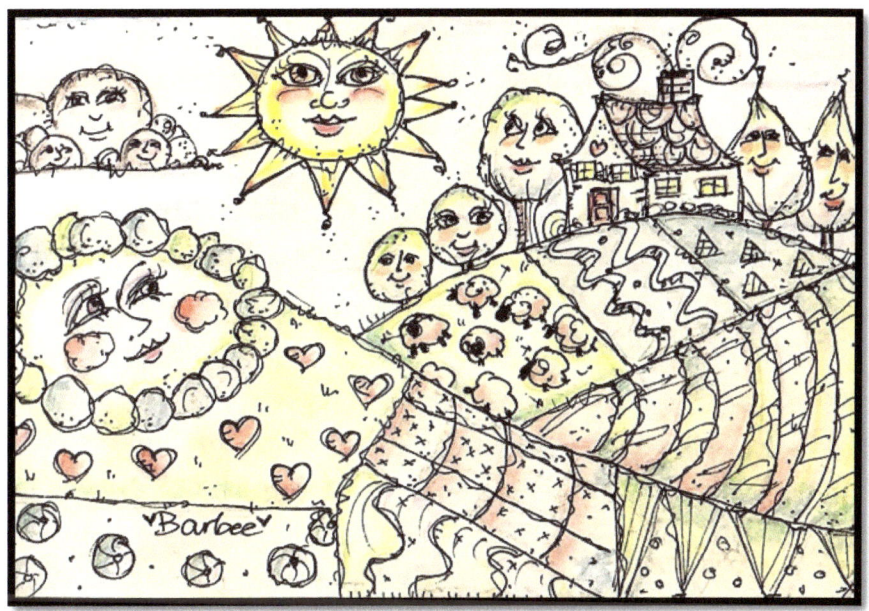

32 for 2 July: DESERT OR DESSERT

I served up a dish of desert mixed in with ice cream for dessert with a desert backdrop! This depicts spring in the desert so there is a nice pond keeping things wet. I had fun making the stem of this desert goblet/dessert glass, and I added a crowned owl on top of the cactus! My artwork was greatly affected by a French caricaturist from the 1800s known by the pseudonym of Jean-Jacques or J.J. Grandville (born 1803, died 1847). Grandville was his parents' stage name. His fantasy art looks like it was studied by the great artist Salvador Dali! A popular grunge rock band even used his art on their album cover in 1995. I found out about him from a high school friend who's fantasy art I adored. Even though my style is not as complex as his, I owe him thanks for stretching my imagination and helping to give me an artist's license to draw crazy-fun stuff!

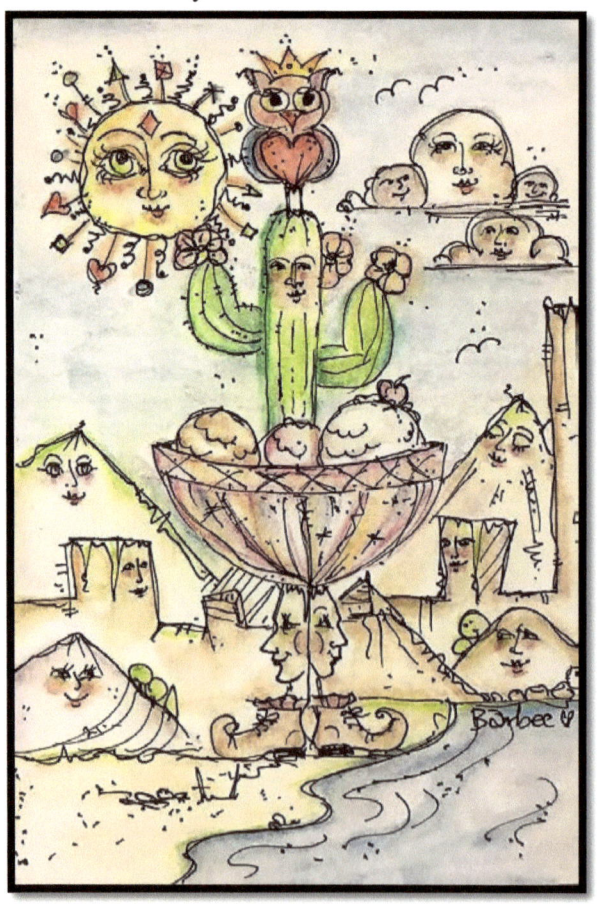

33 for 3 July: ORANGE

Fun times making the letters of the word ORANGE into "things'!" This is a favorite way of mine to practice art while giving my brain a workout - my favorite kind of exercise! Just draw big letters and doodle faces and other body parts in them.

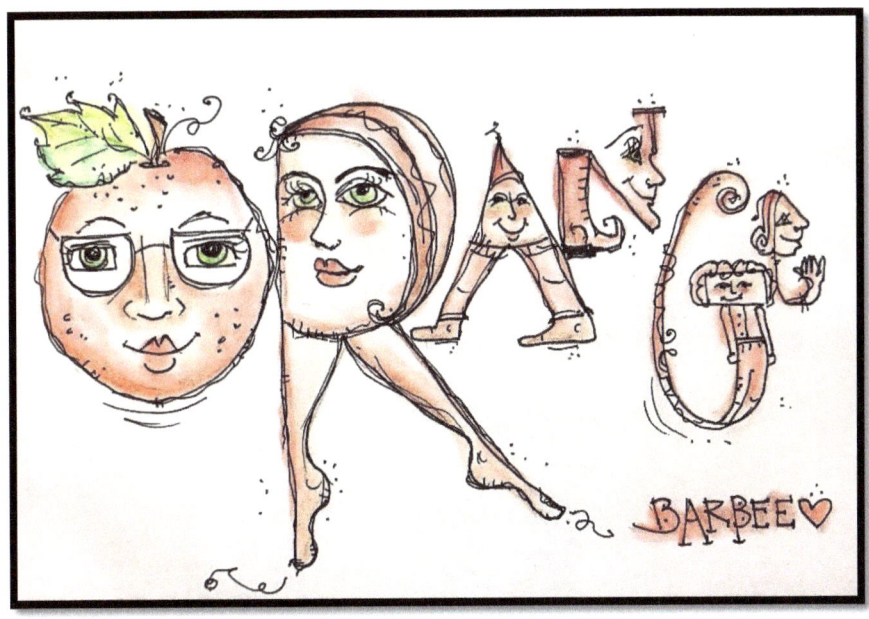

34 for 4 July: 4TH OF JULY

Happy 4th of July/ Independence Day! I love the red, white and blue and I love the U.S.A. A big thank you to everyone around the world who helps us stay a great nation because we certainly don't do anything alone.

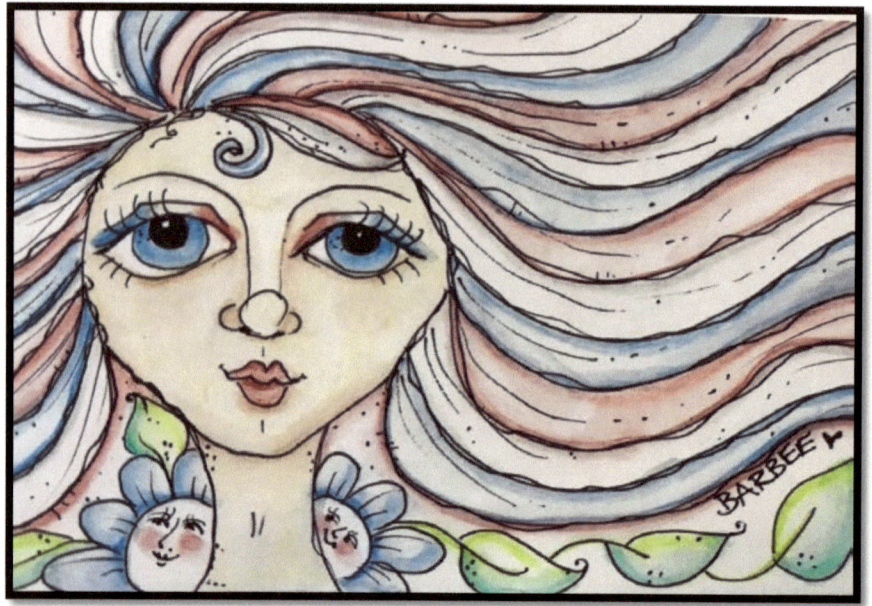

35 for 5 July: FAVORITE APPLE

What's my favorite kind of apple? An apple with a face, ha-ha! I like them green, too, so it was hard trying to separate the leaves from the apples but I tried by using different colors of green and adding flowers for variety at the bottom.

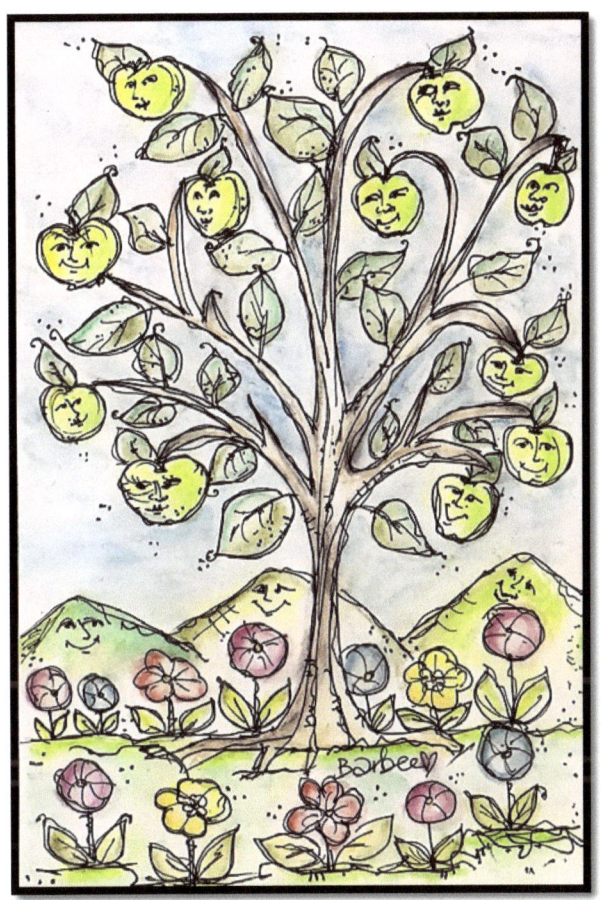

36 for 6 July: PERFUME

In the beginning, I wanted to do a sort of grid of fragrant flowers and did not want to do perfume bottles! Somehow, the bottles spoke to me and demanded equal time with the flowers, ha-ha! Drawing or collaging things in grids is another fun way to get lots of art on a page.

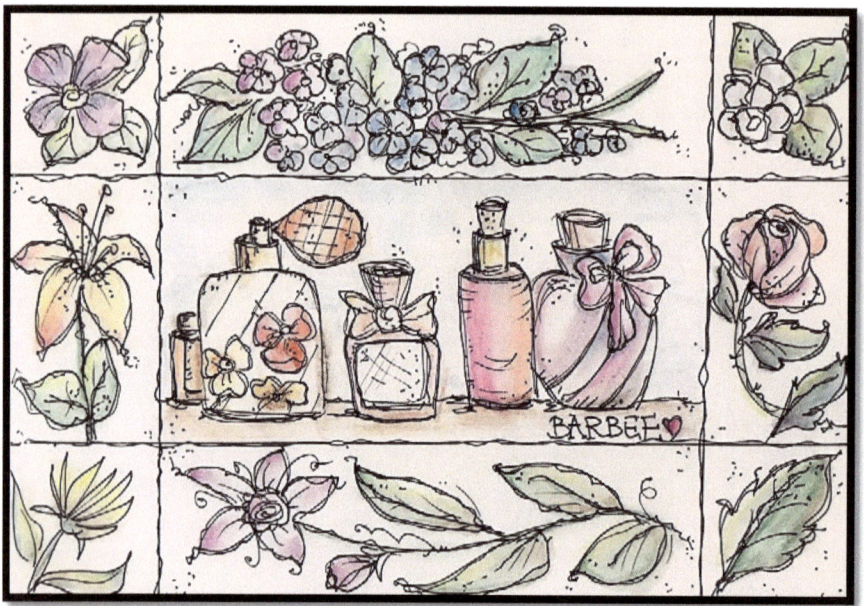

37 for 7 July: KAOMOJI OR EMOJI

I volunteered two new emojis on this 4x6 inch index card to meet the challenge of this prompt. First, my "Frida Flower" inspired by Frida Kahlo, a wonderfully brilliant artist born in Mexico. Second, my version of a Picasso-style "Pi-cats-oh." I think each of them expresses an idea! Both these magnificent, expressive artists continue to have a tremendous influence on us, years after their deaths. I'd recommend watching some internet videos on each of these ultra-interesting people to anyone interested in our art and culture.

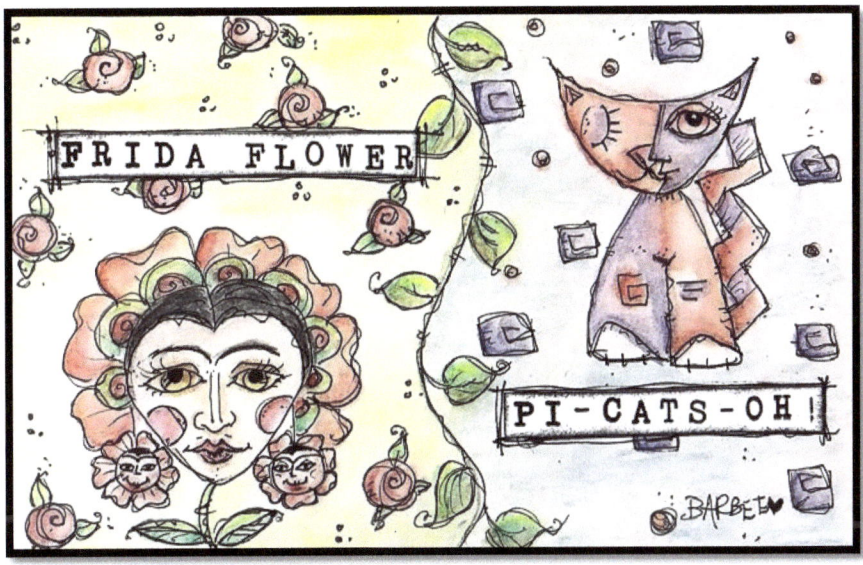

38 for 8 July: CHARCOAL

It reads: If life gives you charcoal, make diamonds. I remembered hearing somewhere that we can make diamonds from charcoal, so I researched and found a dear husband who'd made his loving wife tiny diamonds using just a few ingredients including a microwave oven that heats up the ingredients for over 99 minutes. He ended up with very tiny diamonds covered in soot - not the best quality. He placed them in resin and created a necklace which he gave his wife for their anniversary. How sweet, but I'd prefer diamonds of the size below although they'd probably weigh down my ears too much.

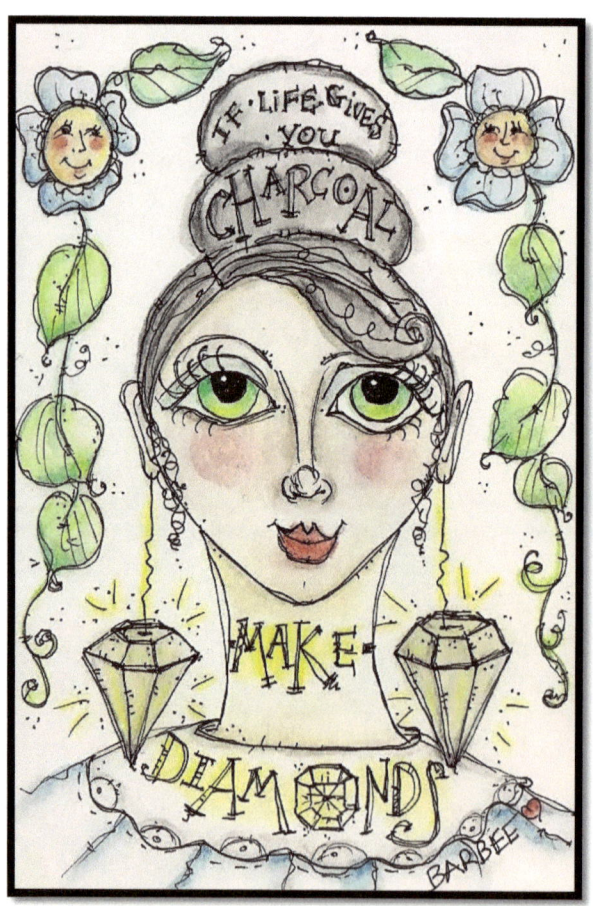

39 for 9 July: AMPERSAND

What to do with an ampersand? Give it a face and make it dance, of course! I also added random stamps and "ampersand" flowers! I enjoy drawing stylized anatomy. If I wanted to make perfectly shaped people, I'd trace them, but wonky ones are way too much fun! &&&&&&&&&&

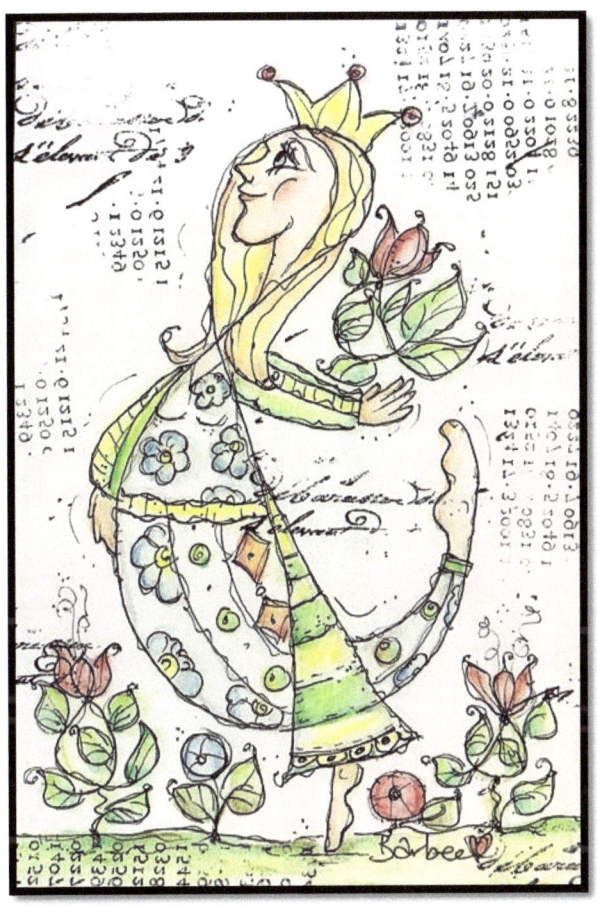

40 for 10 July: STEAMPUNK

I love steampunk so was happy about this prompt as it assisted me in trying out some new-to-me techniques. I rummaged around my supplies and located this die-cut butterfly, 2 small paper flowers, metal buttons, gears and charms plus some die cut corner embellishments and gems, then added texture paste and paint to create this piece. I topped it off with a tiny skull and a key.

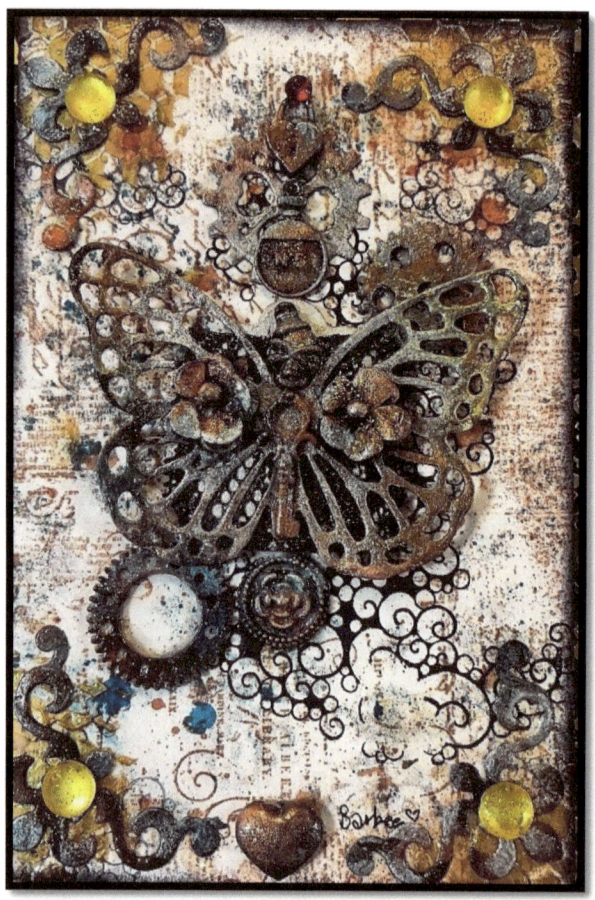

41 for 11 July: ROOTS

"...and little did they know, as silly as they were, that the roots controlled the waves and wind, as well as the clouds and weather!" This is a quote from my new book, although it'll be a while before I release it, as I'm enjoying the art of it too much. I knew for the prompt ROOTS, I'd have to draw trees but wanted to show their global importance and connection so showed them firmly planted in the world. Do you notice what her cheeks are made of? More trees, of course!

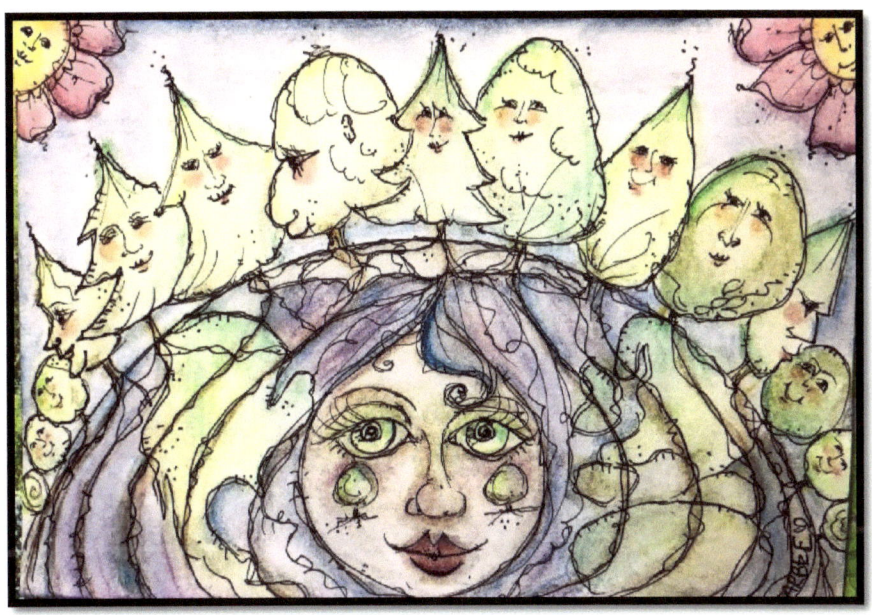

42 for 12 July: ONOMATOPOEIA

This prompt is such an interesting, long, hard-to-pronounce word! Definition of ONOMATOPOEIA: a word that mimics the sound it represents. I wanted to draw a Happy Cat, so drew it (and its friends) and chose my word "CA-CHING," imagining that the lucky cat might be a sort of slot machine. I hope it's obvious that these cats are also quite happy!

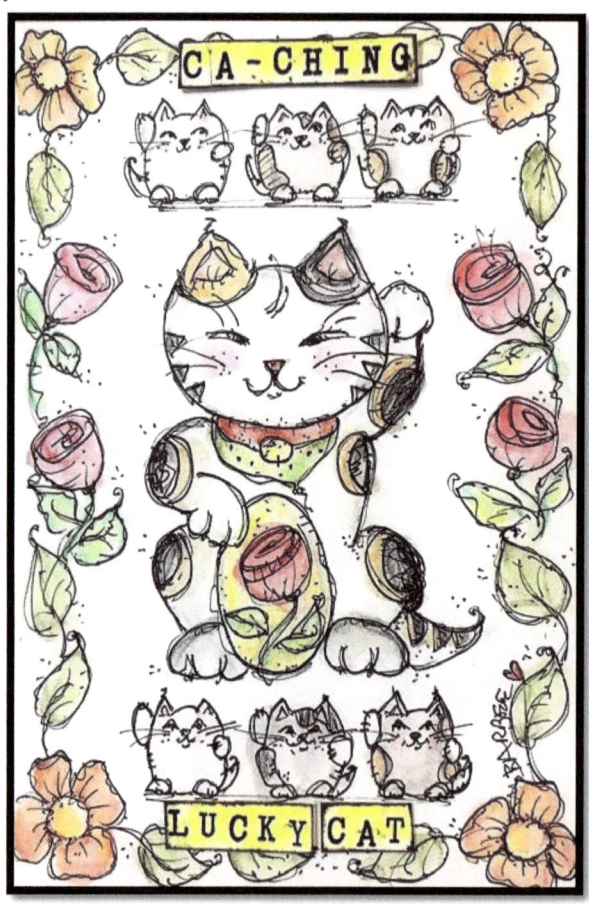

43 for 13 July: LYRICS

More than a decade ago, my dear husband and I stopped for after-work drinks at a beautiful restaurant called Tom Ham's Lighthouse on San Diego's "Harbor Island," not really an island, but rather a small strip of land jutting out into the Harbor. A very talented older lady started playing the piano and singing. I asked if she knew a song from the 1940s or 50s about a house on a street and I hummed a bit of the tune that was in my head. She asked me lots of questions - like who sang it, etc. but all I could remember was that tiny piece of the tune! We decided to stay for dinner as she tried various songs from that bygone era. Then, she got it: "Knowing I'm on the Street Where You Live!" I was so happy and grateful! I love music and played guitar in my youth, so I was ecstatic to hear that little tune come to life! The beauty of the surroundings, the happiness I felt with my sweet husband, the food and, to top it off, this amazing entertainer, made this night magical and one of my favorite evenings EVER!! I drew a whimsical lilac tree and lark with a house in a tree that are on that street, well, at least in my head!

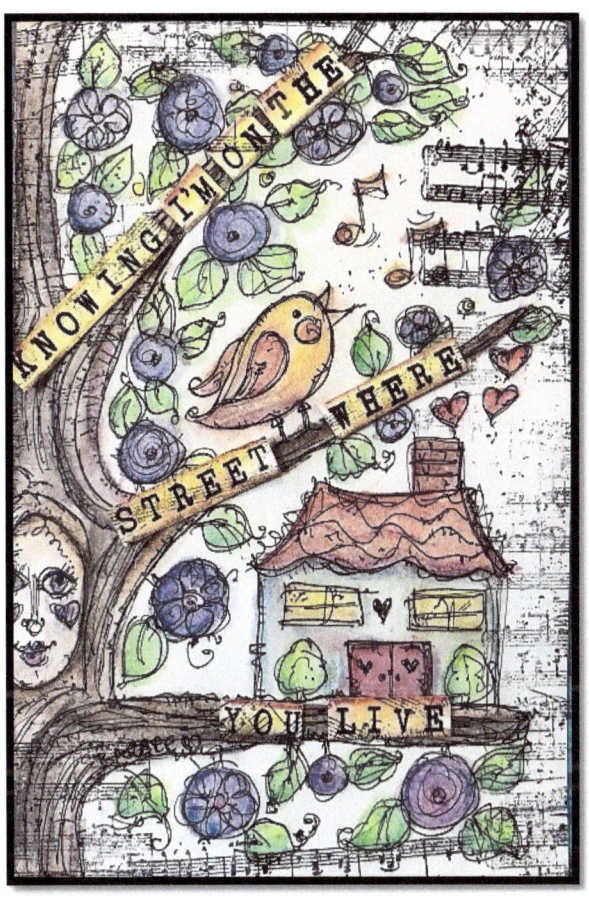

44 for 14 July: DENIM OR BLUE

I created a blue cat being admired by the sun for this BLUE prompt. He's happily holding his green fish-friend. I've heard that blue cats have to be male! Just another interesting fantasy factoid that I dreamed up while creating this happy trio. It goes back to hearing from my veterinarian friend Cora that calico cats must be female (really?)!

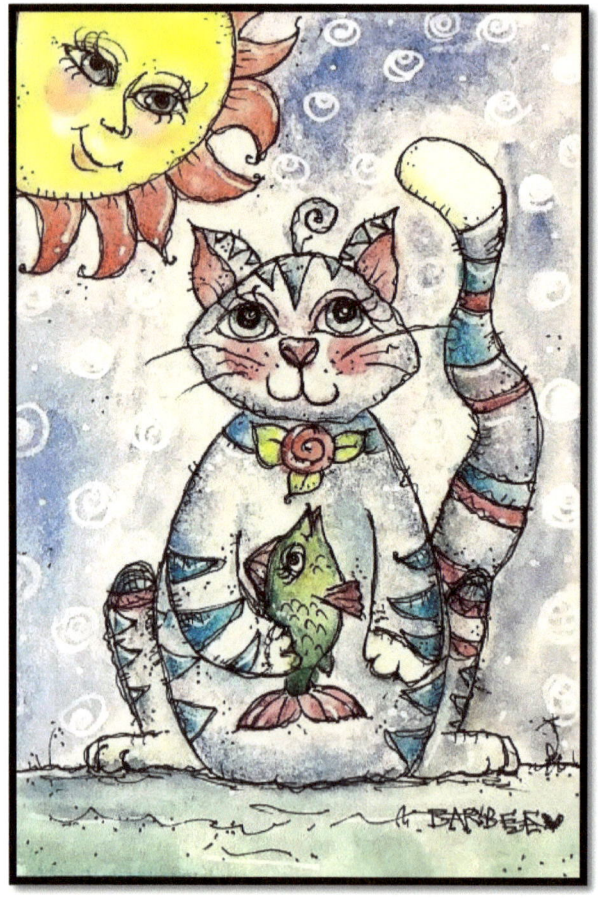

45 for 15 July: NIGHT SKY

For the prompt NIGHT SKY, I wanted to create the night sky with a reference point so painted an earth scene with a moon and starry, starry night. Someone needs to wake up that moon so he can enjoy it too!

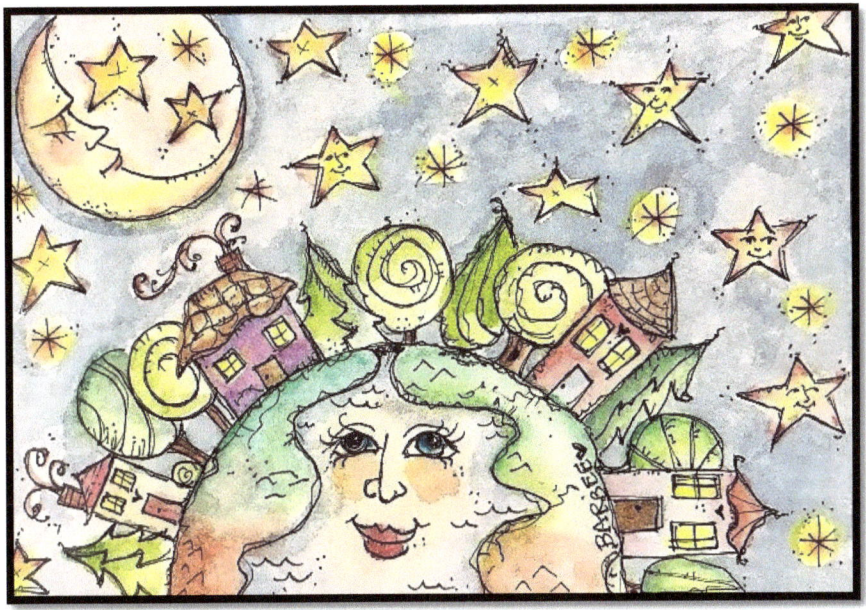

46 for 16 July: LOVE

I made a simple, curvy-lined hummingbird with a little quote to fit the prompt: "Hummingbirds Carry Love." It's a fun hummingbird to create and was one of the most fun to color.

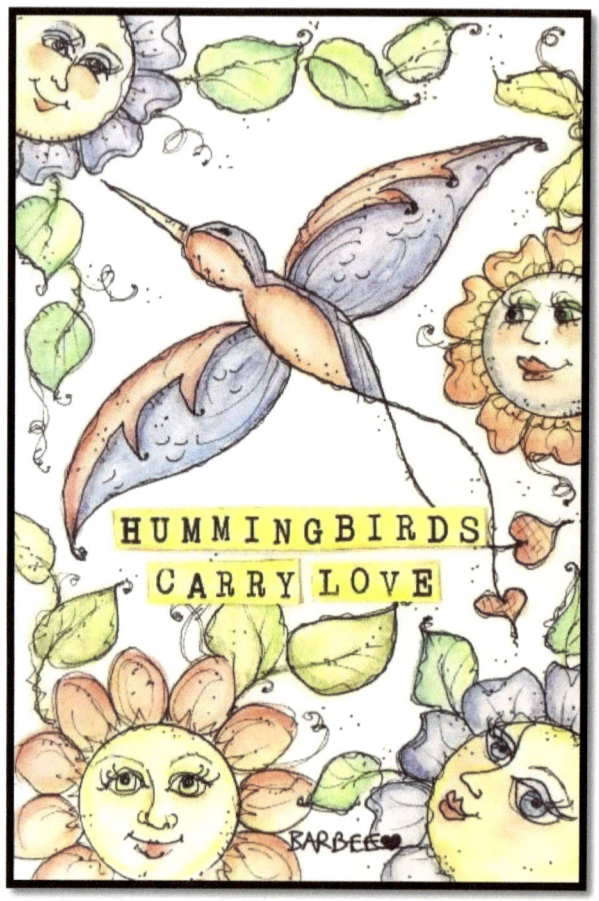

47 for 17 July: LAYERS

I added these words to a heavily layered index card I made: "Love Powers the Gears of the Heart." It has a piece of vintage writing as its foundation adhered with matte medium. I added scrolled corners, gears and other shapes die cut out of glitter and metallic cardstock. I also die cut a heart out of white cardstock then drew a face and hair with a black liner .01 pen. I colored the heart-face drawing with watercolor pencils and added a light text stamp. I added gold texture paste through a small stencil around the edges. I finished the card using black archival stamp pad ink applied with a makeup sponge to make it look distressed/antique. Mixed media is a fun form of art that incorporates different media, textures and layers.

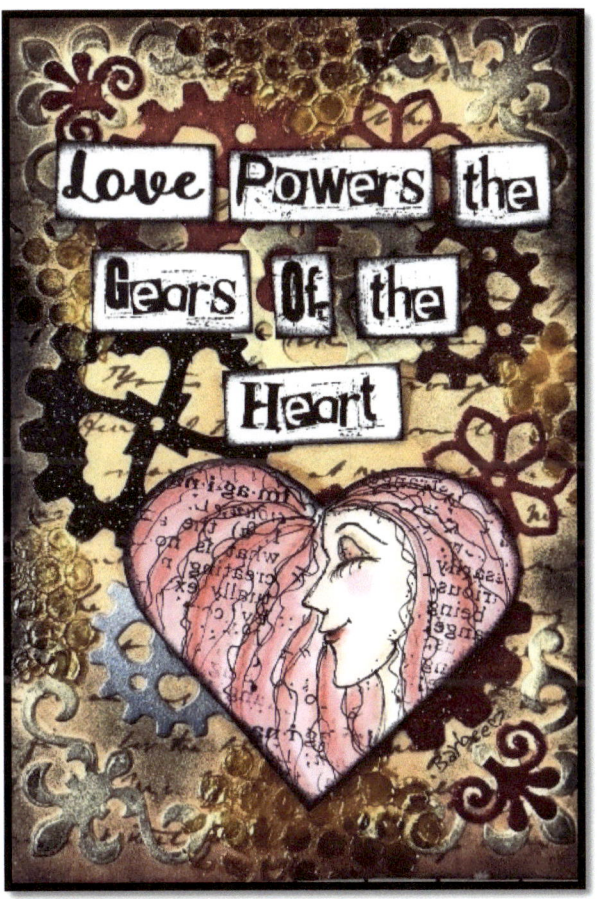

48 for 18 July: INTERSECTION

I enjoy arting with letters, numbers and words so printed the prompt INTERSECTION with some letters, then added flowers, leaves and other designs that I felt portrayed the prompt. This is one of my secret tricks to catch up when I'm behind on doing daily art or lack for ideas. I find that just printing the prompt word, then adding doodles, gives me something I can complete quickly and still enjoy the challenge.

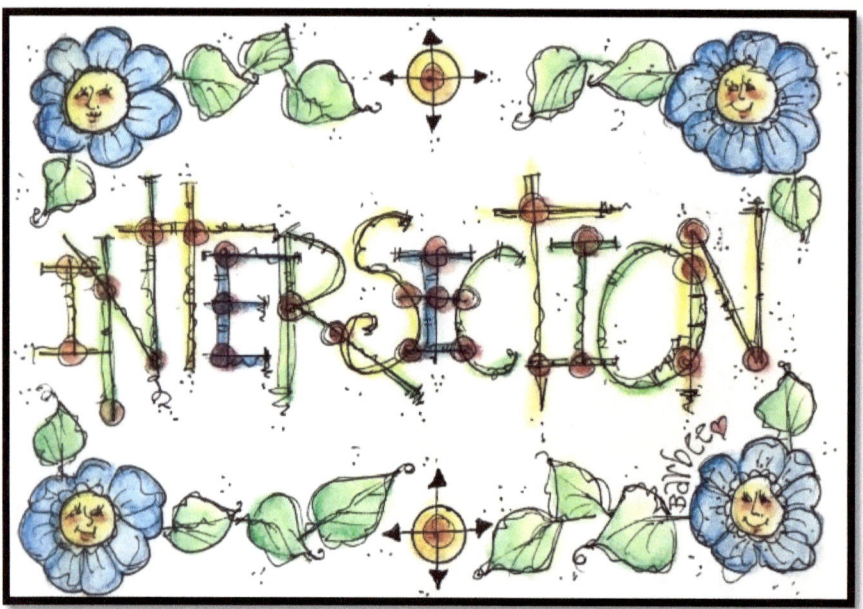

49 for 19 July: CHARM BRACELET

I wanted to feature the amazing, controversial entertainer, Mae West, most popular in the 1930s, but who's career spanned decades, so it took me a bit longer than usual to do some research on her. I enjoyed every minute of learning about her and recommend everyone read about her fascinating life. I adorned this card with little pearls, gems and flowers to make it more "Mae."

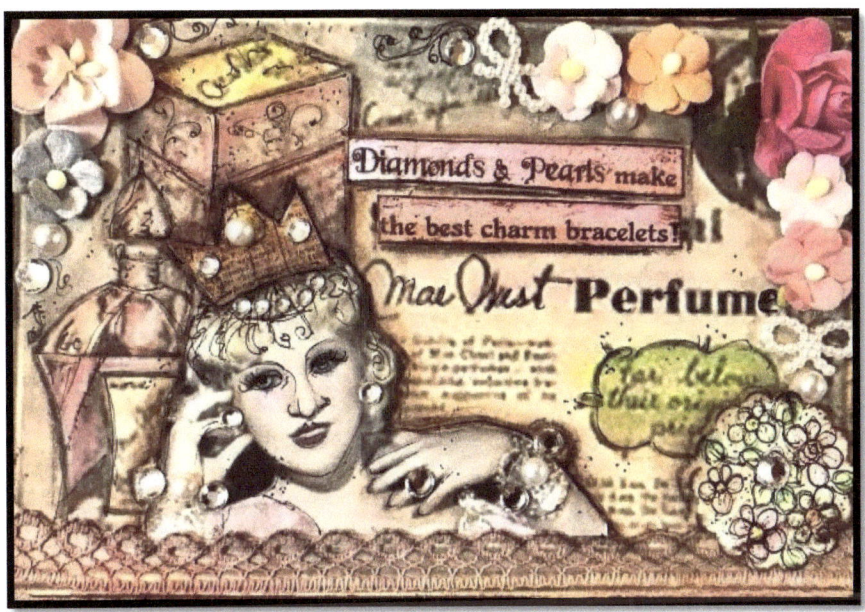

50 for 20 July: SUN OR MOON (2-CAT NIGHT)

I look forward to evenings, when my wonderful husband and I have a small dinner and watch our beautiful big flat screen TV. Our two cats, once Ferrell kittens, used to sit on my lap and enjoy the evenings too. Their warmth and gentle purring was soothing and comforting. Because of this, I call nights when I'm cold or aching "two cat nights," ha-ha!! For this prompt, I drew these sweet cats outside under the moon (although in reality, they were full-time indoor cats). I used my artist license to add a bit more color to them.

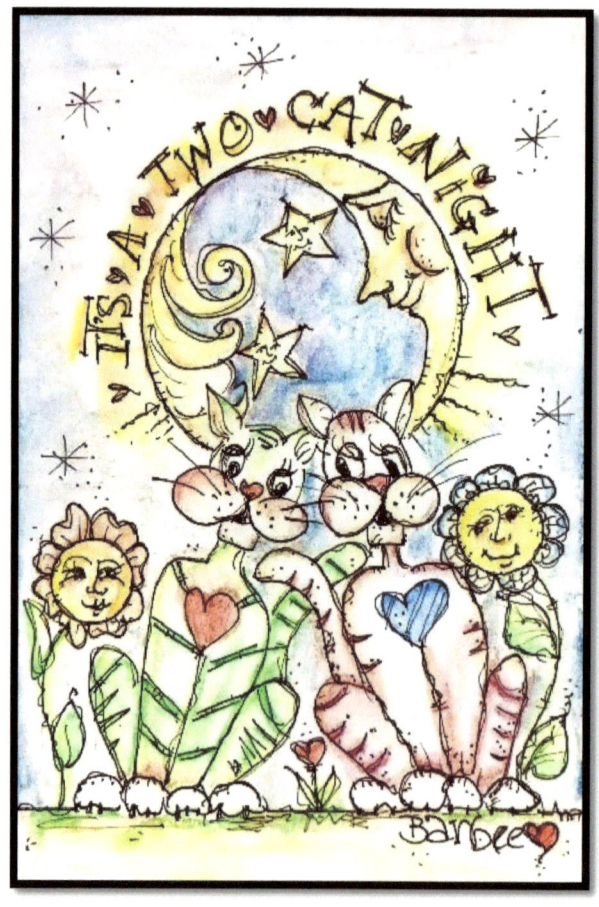

51 for 21 July: SWIM (FISHBOWL)

For the prompt SWIM, I drew a fish-shaped bowl with a fun interior design. Notice the cat lurking on the bottom? The fish are very curious about him and are swimming closer to have a better look, much to his delight!

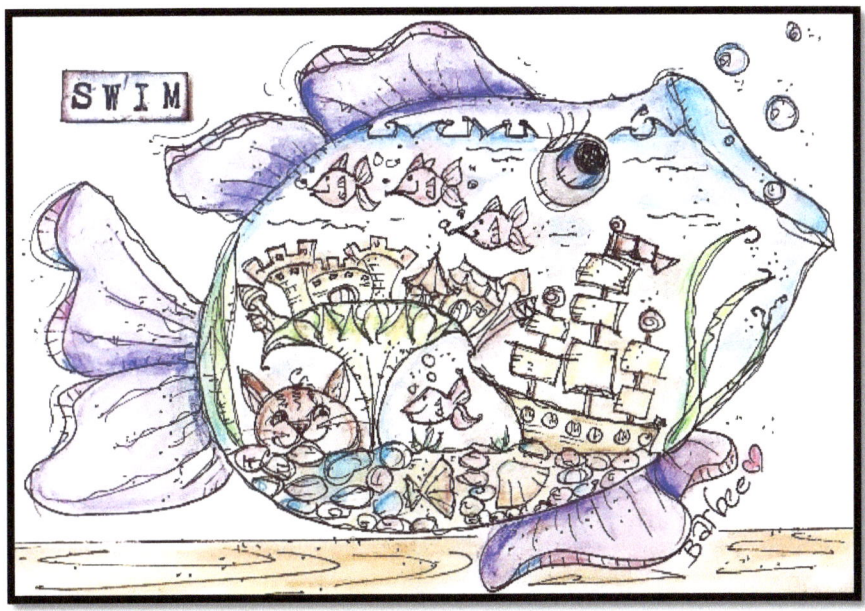

52 for 22 July: ADJECTIVE

I found an adjective for each letter of the word "adjective" and tried to decorate each word accordingly!

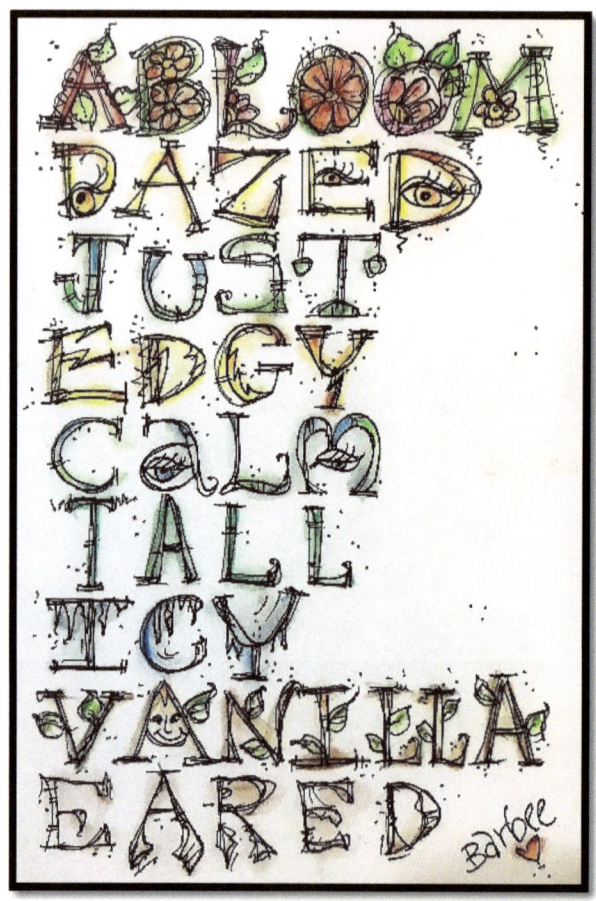

53 for 23 July: MIRROR

I die cut a mirror shape that resembled one I had when I was a teen. This side is a wonkily-pretty, crowned young woman who's smiling in the mirror oddly, because of what she really looks like which is much scarier than the one in the mirror in another prompt. It's so nice that this is what people see when they look at her! Look ahead at #56 to see what she REALLY looks like.

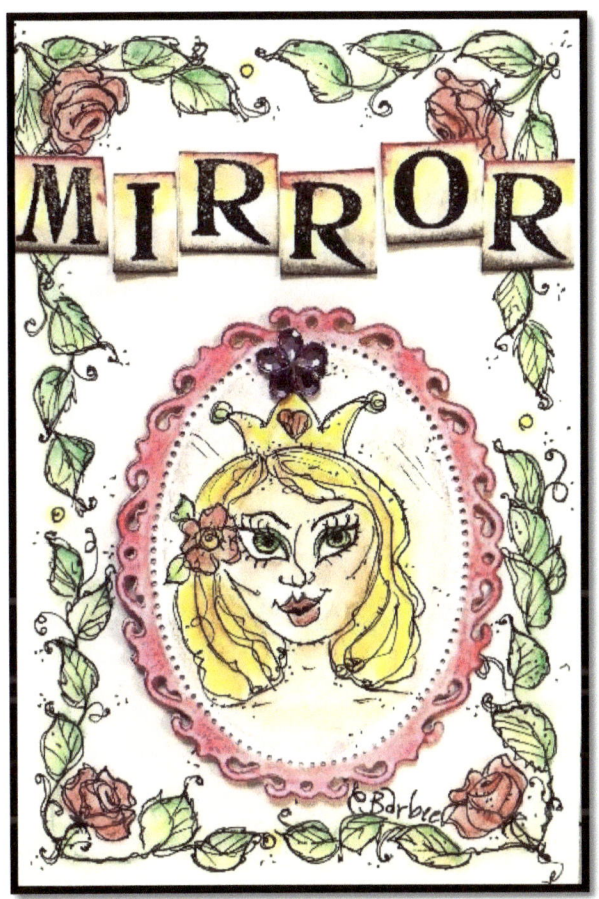

54 for 24 July: GREETINGS FROM

One of the many things I'm enjoying about this year's wonderful ICAD creative challenge is being able to re-do art pieces on larger 4x6 inch size cards. I'm keeping lessons-learned in mind. I took the opportunity to re-create a previous year's ICAD for this prompt and am happier with the way it turned out. The bird and butterfly are little stamps and I enjoyed making this tiny greeting card that actually opens.

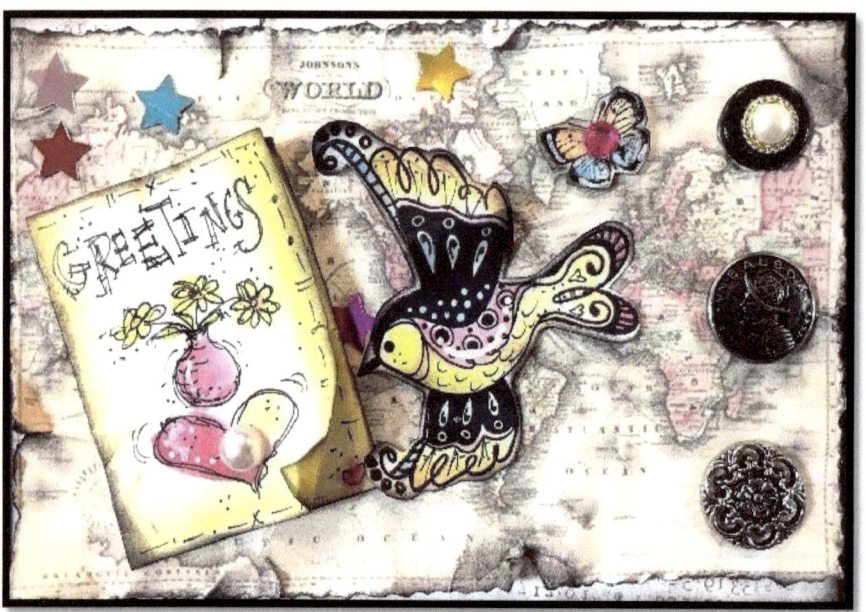

55 for 25 July: SEPIA (EYES)

I struggled with this prompt a bit but remembered that my dear husband has fabulous brown eyes. Just about every day I remember taking our wedding vows in the Philippines because fate and the military took us there and that's where we decided to get married!

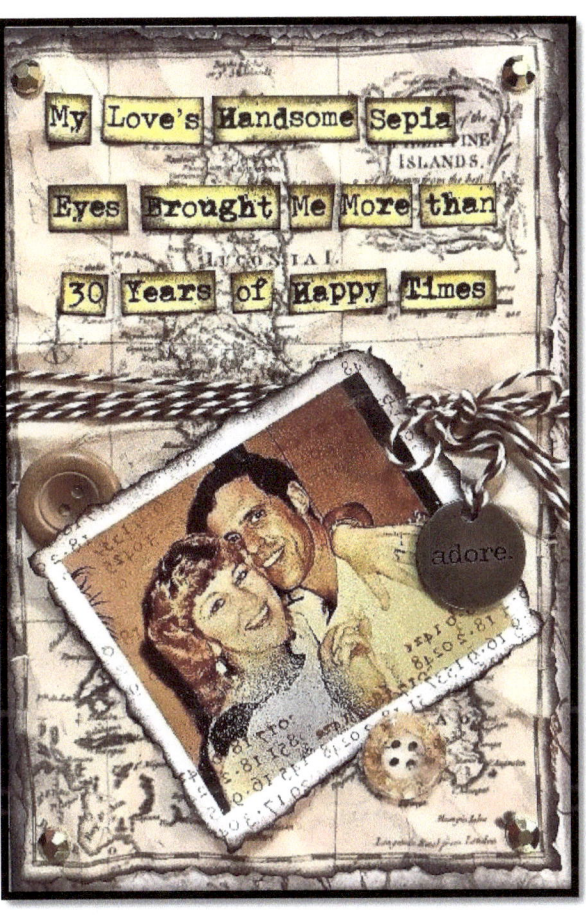

When I looked into his beautiful brown eyes during the ceremony, I saw the promise of a wonderful future but had no idea how much happiness this wonderful man would bring me. His eyes were gorgeous that day and held me captive with their glow. I thank the dear Lord that the events that led us to that far off island occurred and I've never looked back. So, I used a filter in this photo from that day and found a vintage sepia map of the Philippines to distress as a foundation. I used a data stamp for the base index card to add texture. I also pressed that little data stamp onto the photo for fun and added the stamped medal note that describes in one word my feelings for him – "adore."

56 for 26 July: GHOST OR ZOMBIE

This is what my wonky MIRROR lady (from card #53) looks like when she looks in the mirror, although others see her as I drew her in card #53. Definitely a zombie, and the first I've ever attempted - do you think she resembles a zombie? Well, maybe a person becoming a zombie?

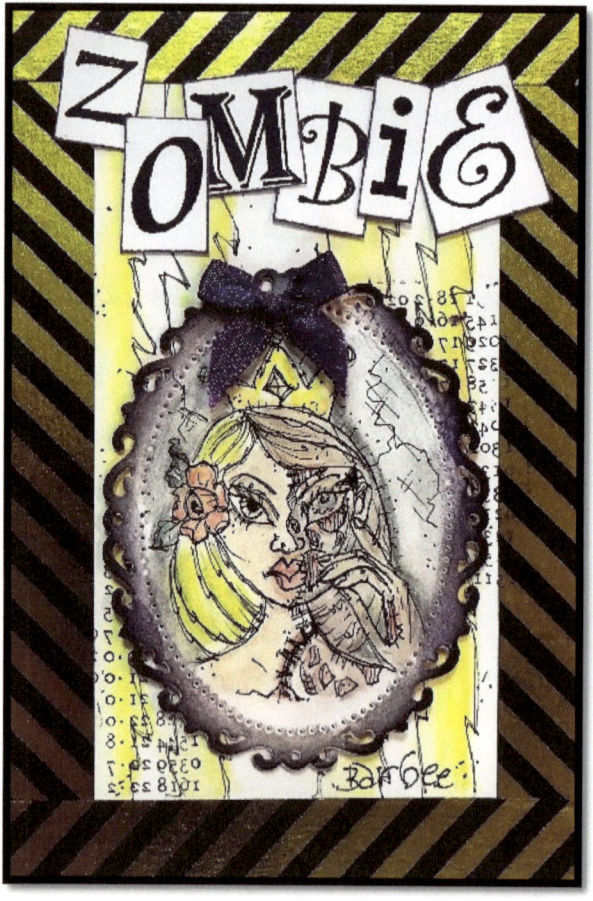

57 for 27 July: SPRING

I created an index card in a previous year where I wrote the word WINTER in cursive and drew a winter scene. I was urged then by one of my FaceBook friends to do a set portraying all the seasons. Because of her, I decided to do something similar with this prompt for SPRING, as well as with the next prompts that are the rest of the seasons. I enjoyed adding lots of bright spring color with watercolor (ink) pencils! They give a vivid color and don't reactivate if they get wet again like normal watercolor pencils.

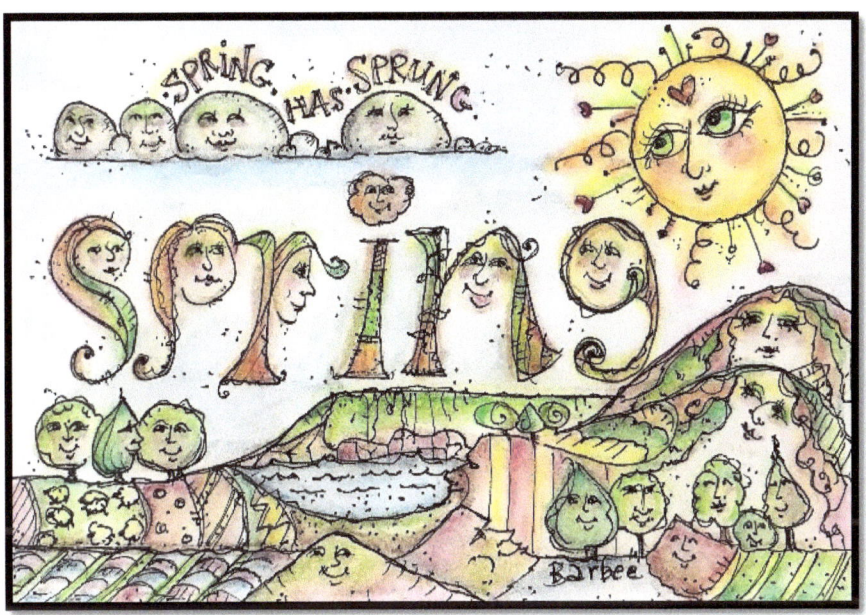

58 for 28 July: SUMMER

This is similar to card #57 SPRING, although I changed the scene and colors a bit to reflect the season.

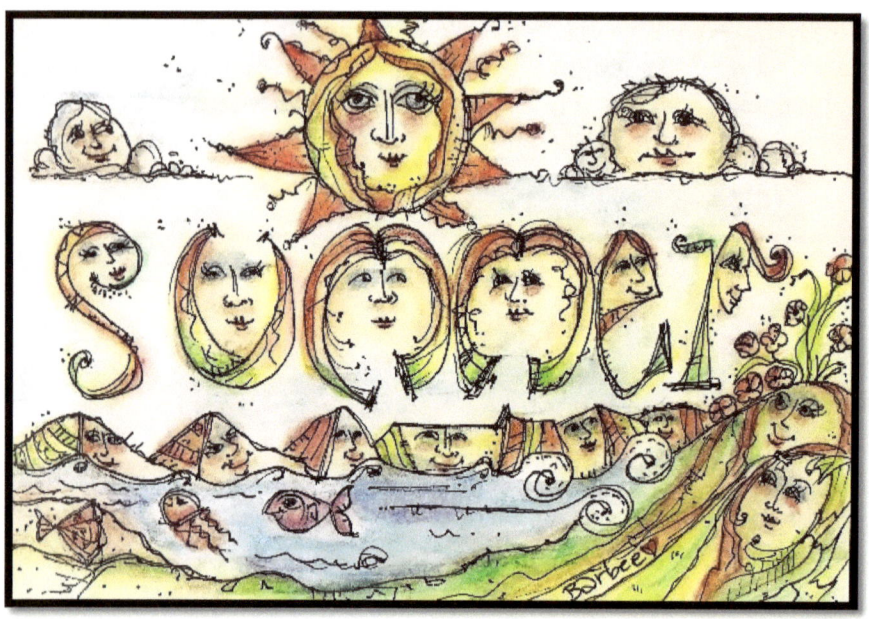

59 for 29 July: AUTUMN

This is similar to the previous two cards, #57 SPRING, and #58 SUMMER.

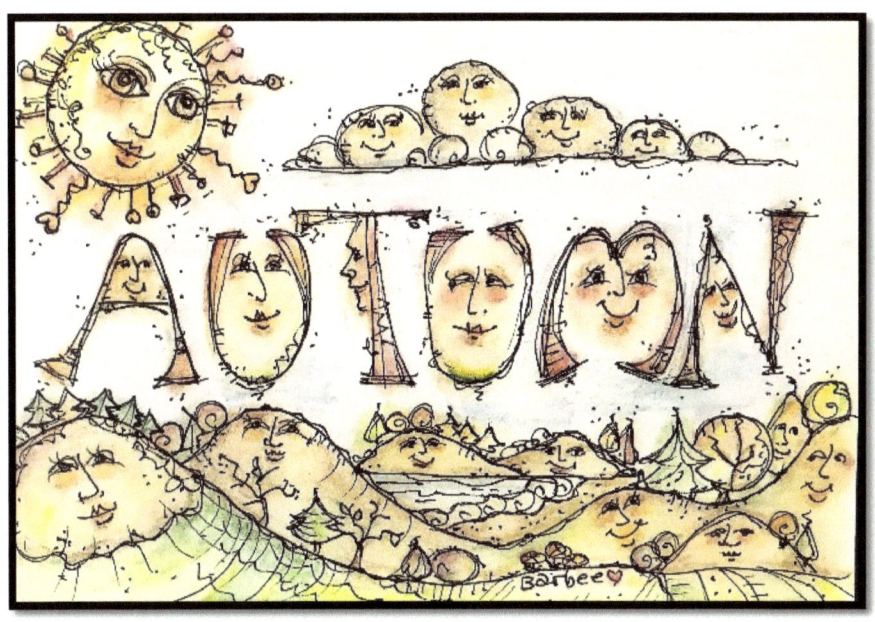

60 for 30 July: WINTER

This is similar to the previous three cards, #57 SPRING, #58 SUMMER, and #59 AUTUMN, and together, the 4 make a nice little set of the 4 seasons.

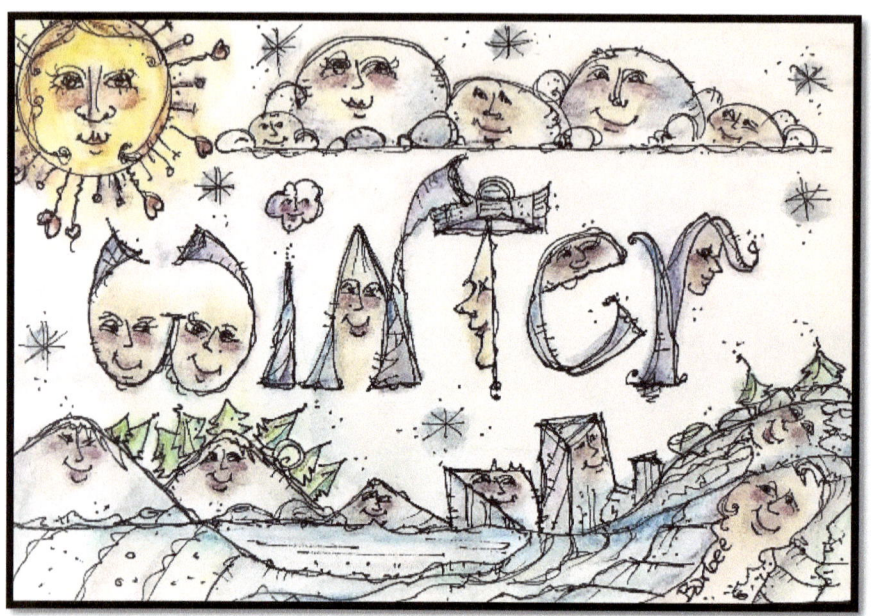

61 for 31 July: SUNSET

This was the last index card for the summer of 2017. I continue to create art and post it in several Facebook Groups, including the wonderful ICAD creative challenge. It's an inspirational, safe place to share my "Happy Art" with other, like-minded artists. I wish to thank all the friendly, sweet, encouraging and inspiring artists who participated in that ICAD Challenge and especially our leader, teacher guru and friend, Tammy Garcia, and her extraordinary moderators/admin ladies. I wrote a note of gratitude on the last index card and another in this little poem that applies to my readers, as well:

The sun is setting on ICAD 2017.
This is the 61st index card I've done.
Happiness and love I feel for everyone!
The talented artists who so freely gave
likes and comments on my art - YOU made me feel brave.
And to our talented ICAD Guru, Tammy, of Daisy Yellow,
a great big THANK YOU for your time and talent
- YOU are one in a MILLION!

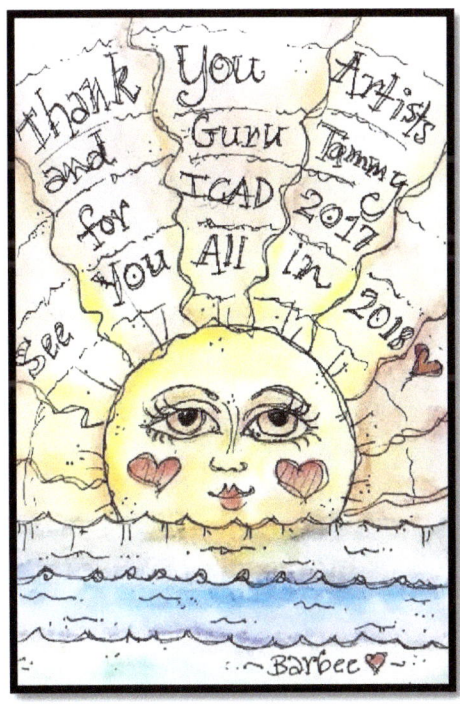

I hope you enjoyed my first book! I also hope you've added your share of doodling in the blank areas of this book and that you learn to be happy with your art – it's a wonderful way to escape from life's worries, but still enjoy its challenges!

www.ingramcontent.com/pod-product-compliance
Lightning Source LLC
Chambersburg PA
CBHW040230220526
45473CB00001B/181